To Irmeli
This book is dedicated in honour of my wife,
who has faithfully stood at my side.
Fight the good fight of faith
Never give up, and always saw new possibilities.
Have always had the joy, despite much physical pain.
She held out to the last and has now reached her goal in life.
An eternal life with Jesus.
Irmeli, we shall meet in heavenly places.

Proverbs 18:22
Whoso findeth a wife findeth a good thing and obtaineth favour of the LORD.

The Tales of a Salesman
by
Curt Larsson

2019 Curt Larsson
Förlag: BoD – Books on Demand, Stockholm, Sverige
Tryck: BoD – Books on Demand, Norderstedt, Tyskland
ISBN: 978-91-7463-324-5

Contents

My life in Sweden
- Beginning as a salesman — 8
- My first visit to the church — 10
- Industrial school in Västerås — 11
- First meeting with Irmeli — 13
- Military service at F16 — 14
- Door to door in Västerås — 16
- Door to door in Stockholm — 16
- Employment at Olivetti — 18
- I married Irmeli — 19
- Moved to Trollhättan 1967 — 20
- Talked about Australia — 21

Migrating to Australia
- Emigration to Australia — 22
- Boat trip with Achille Lauro — 22
- Bonegilla — 27
- Train ride to Sydney — 29
- Employment at Olivetti — 31
- Moving to our first apartment — 35
- Facing a shotgun — 37
- Thoughts of return to Sweden — 40
- Places in NSW — 42

Migrating back to Sweden
- Going back to Sweden — 48
- Return to Australia with — 50
- Moving to Killara — 52
- Trevor and Birgitta visiting — 53
- Moving to Harbord — 54
- Puppy Dog Danny Boy — 56
- Trevor and Birgitta re-visit — 57
- Holidays in Bali — 58
- Irmeli's parents emigrate — 61

	Vacation in Queensland	61
	Our caravan in flood	62
	New apartment in Allawah	66
	Joe's temptations	68
The most significant change in my life	My life transformation	71
	Decision for Christ	75
	Travel to Sweden June 1978	77
	Struck by lightening at church	79
	An agent enters the store	80
	Prophecy in church	80
	Repair of gear box free	81
	Sauna competition	84
	Miriam and Kjell emigrating	85
	Dealing with Dennis	86
	Big order of dishes	87
	Mark is starting to work	90
	Trip to Sweden via Hawaii	92
	Journey with Jouko to WA	94
	The tall Peter	98
	Healed from noose bleeding	98
	Healed from gallstone attacks	100
	Riding on the back of a truck	102
	School holidays in Cairns	102
	Olivetti agency	103
Our greatest difficulties	1984 a year of sorrow	105
	Robert dies	108
	Travel to the funerals	111
	Elida	111
	Conference in Halmstad	113
	More sad news	113
	The van is on fire	113

	Bought Toyota Coaster bus	115
	Toyota Coaster Bus stolen	117
	Satan worshippers found	118
	Limited Edition by Kevin Best	121
	Bible missions into Russia	124
	Gold Coast with Anneli	125
	Hiring of new salesman	124
	Bloodbath in Mt. Isa	129
	Journey with Kjell to Darwin	130
	Outi returns to Sweden	133
Ministering	Mission trip Philippines	134
	Import paintings from China	138
	Bible smuggling to Xiamen	139
	Bible smuggling Guangzhou I	139
	Bible smuggling Guangzhou II	141
	Bible smuggling to Shanghai	142
Back to business	The silk flowers come	144
	The vicar comes	147
	Travel to Sweden and Finland	148
	Travel to Tumut	150
	Irmeli fell in front of truck	151
	The sale of our company	151
	Selling our unit in Sydney	153
Return to Sweden	Irmeli goes to the Lord	155
	Prayer of salvation!	159
	Prayer	159
About the author	About the author	160

My life in Sweden
Beginning as a salesman

Me, Miriam and Lisbeth

I was born in Ulricehamn the 15th of July 1944. Before my birth, my mother Märta, was praying that my father, Herman, would get some help with Miriam, their oldest daughter, who was nearly two years old. My father was a miller and had a lot of work at the water mill in the middle of July. A Christian lady from Småland, which is the neighbouring state, got a word from the Lord, that someone in Ulricehamn is about to give birth, and needed help. This lady went by train to Ulricehamn and went to the local bakery, near the station. She said that she had come to help a lady who was about to give birth. They said that there was no one here that fits that description, but just a few kilometres north of town, the millers' wife Märta Larsson was about to give birth. She arrived on the 14th of July. And I was born the day after the 15th of July.

My sales life started at about 9 years of age when I felt that I needed a little more money to move with. So I took the train to Storms Fröhandel in Skara (seed business), Sweden, and said that I wanted to buy some seeds to sell to the farmers where I lived. I got a discount of 30%. I traded for all my money and went home to Marbogården's mill where my family and I lived. I started cycling out to the nearest peasants and knocking on the doors. I told them that I sell flower and vegetable seeds. And it was always the housewife that opened the door. The sales went well, and I renegotiated my discount, and I got a 50% discount, then I earned more money.

In the autumn I expanded my sales to Christmas magazines, which also went very well, and I won my first box camera in a sales competition. Sales were up and running, until the summer, then I went to Skara where they had markets with various amusements and ice cream sales. I checked out with an ice cream company, if I could get an ice cream box, such one that you hang around the neck. I got the job and were given a fully stocked ice cream box. I did not wait for anyone to come to me and buy ice cream, but went to people and said "here are ice cream sticks" "come and buy ice cream sticks". It didn't take long before it was time to re-stock. I had some competition in that market, by another ice cream company, and the manager noticed that I was selling well and asked me if I could "join them" I said yes. But the first company wanted me back, and I let them fight over me, then I moved back to the first ice cream company.

My first visit to the church

Miriam, Herman, Lisbeth, Märta and me

My parents had sold the mill, and we moved to Hasslösa in Sweden, which was the neighbouring shire. My Mother was involved in the Salvation Army and father used to go with her from time to time. But we frequented the Swedish Church during my upbringing. Sometimes I had difficulty to keep awake in the church, but it was better in the Salvation Army. My sister Miriam and I once went to a tent meeting in Vinninga.

After the meeting, some ladies came to us and asked if they could pray with me. I couldn't say no, so they prayed with me! When we got home, Miriam said that I had been saved. But then life continued for me as usual. I had not had any experience that I can remember from that time. However, I started to play the snare drum in the Salvation Army in Skara. I remember once when I marched with them playing the drum on the streets in Skara. And also at their meetings in the corps, someone used to stand up and say something about their faith. I didn't understand anything about it.

Industrial school in Västerås

I continued with many sales until I left school at the age of 14. Then my mother told me that I had to get a profession, selling is no profession, she said. I wasn't so keen on it, but I let myself be persuaded. My mother applied to Asea Industrial School in Västerås. The application was accepted, so I and Janne, my cousin, went to Västerås to do a test. The test I thought was quite simple, and after the test, we went to his brothers Sune, Lars and Rolf in Stockholm. Then it was time to return to our homes. Later we received a letter from Asea that we had been accepted. Janne and I were so disappointed.

But on the 1st of April 1960, we started at the Industrial School, which was a three-year school. I had chosen the mechanical line, which meant turning, drilling, grinding, welding, soldering, winding of stators and rotors. Janne wants the electric range.

I lived in a boy's boarding house, Normanseth, on Gideonsbergsgatan. Janne stayed at another boy's boarding house on the floor above. At the long weekends, we went to my cousins in Stockholm, in the beginning, they picked us up. But then I asked my mother who was the guardian of my savings account if I could withdraw the money and buy myself a moped. She approved it, and I bought a motorbike. Janne had also bought a moped.

We decided that we would go to Stockholm next long weekend. It started well, and we could only ride at 30 km/h. But at the mid-distance, my moped stopped, so Janne had to tow me. So our journey went even slower. We arrived at Sundbyberg late in the evening and knocked at Sune's flat who lived there, and we stayed overnight with him. I think we got help from Rolf who had a truck and drove us back to Västerås after the weekend. My cousins in Stockholm were always very kind, friendly and helpful.

At the boy's home, I lived with Birger, who was from Umeå. He bought a car, and it was in the winter, then they would go out and try his vehicle. But it was tragic because they had a car accident, where Curt who also went with them died. I felt morbid at the boy's home, an empty place at the dinner table.

I finished school in 1963 and was then a friend of Lennart from Kvänum. We moved together and shared an apartment on Vargbogatan 9 in Västerås. I continued to work at Asea as a turner at the Mimer factory. It was an 8-inch Köping lathe. The boys from the school also worked with the cars they had bought. It was mostly old American cars. Lennart bought a Chevrolet Bel Air 1955, which we used. I had to help them to machine their brake drums in the evenings.

First meeting with Irmeli

Krister at the top right, lower fr. left Kenneth, Lennart

I had a friend called Krister, and we decided to go down to the railway station and check if there were any girls there. We sat in the waiting room, and it was quiet for a while until all of a sudden, there was a commotion between two girls and two guys. They argued about something, we said that if it were going to be trouble, we would go up and make peace. But then the guys went away. Then we went to the girls and wondered what that noise was all about. Well, they had just taken a photo in the photo machine, and while they were waiting for the pictures to come out of the vending machine, the guys appeared and snatched the photos. The girls were Irmeli (who would then become my wife) and Margareta. Afterwards, Krister was going the same way home, so they all went by bus, while I took another bus.

Next day, Krister and I met Irmeli and her friend Margareta on the stairs at Folkets Hus. And from that moment on I developed a keen interest in Irmeli, we

went steady for the next four years.
When the spring came, I looked out through the window in the factory and longed to sell, I did not like this factory work. I asked Irmeli what she thought if I would take up sales again. She said if I felt for it, then I should definitely do it.

Military service at F16 in Uppsala

I watching for intruders

But first, I would do my military service at F16 in Uppsala. It was for 12 months from June 1963. I was a puggmek, (pump aggregate mechanic) who had the task of refuelling the aircraft. I worked with two others, one of them that worked on attaching the hose to the plane and then close the door from outside, a key was stuck in a small wire outside the aircraft.
Once, the wire of the key got stuck between the cockpit door and the key, but he didn't notice it. He signalled his thumbs up to the pilot. Afterwards, they heard on the radio that the pilot had problems with the engine that had stopped. The pilot who was a captain and had a

long experience, and had crashed twice in his service earlier, said in the radio with a very calm voice: "The engine has stopped, I am trying to re-start" he was so quiet that it seemed unnatural. Then he repeated it: "It failed, I try again ... ... it failed, I try again ..... I couldn't start, so I have to jump" then it became silent. The captain steered the aircraft into a forest where the plane crashed. The captain got a ground service after this accident, because the spinal cord becomes shorter by two centimetres for every jump. We then had to go out in fire trucks and walk in the woods among the smoke and extinguish the fire. It was hot and smoky. There were only small pieces left of the plane, except for only one large part, that was the engine.

We also had to go to the shooting range and practice shooting. Once, I had a guy who used to be a little clumsy next to me on the shooting range. He stood on his knees loading a new magazine into the gun, but he held on the shutter button in the meantime, causing him to shoot several shots next to my head where I was lying next to him on my stomach. Thank God for not killing me so I could write this book.

We had to watch around the airfield at night, for intruders, we had orders to shoot sharply at the third warning. One night when I went guard, I heard something, then I became afraid. I called but didn't hear anything. I didn't want to kill anyone. But there was probably an animal inside the airport.

During the long weekends, I went to Västerås and met Irmeli. I used to stay at the Salvation Army Hotel at

Malmaberg, and sometimes it was at the Police Station in the cell, it was free of charge, but you had to take off the strap. Once there was no room, then I slept in the forest. Irmeli went to Glattbrugg in Switzerland and was an au pair at a family for about a year.

Door to door in Västerås

After I had finished my military exercises, I started at Asea again. I got an offer to go to Helsingborg and work on subsistence allowances, ie. Besides the salary, I received a generous contribution for food and room. And then I could enjoy myself a little, but not with girls because I was in love with Irmeli and missed her, so we wrote many letters to each other.
But I longed for a sales job, so I finished at Asea in 1964 and started working as a door knocker at Mobergs Elektriska in Västerås, earning commission only, no basic wage. I worked together with a team that sold white goods. We formed a freezer association, i.e. you could buy what you want and join with about 15 others get a conventional bank loan, which you paid off for a specific time, with a lower interest rate. I was part of a sales team, and we bought a red SAAB 93 together, which we used to go to different cities in Västmanland and sell. The team allowed me to use the car privately if I paid for the petrol.

Door to door in Stockholm

Irmeli worked as a dental nurse in Västerås during that time but got a job at dentist Dahlberg in Stockholm. As a result, I needed to travel far to visit Irmeli, so I applied for a job through the Swedish Public Employment Service in Stockholm. I moved to Hornstull in Stockholm and rented a room. Irmeli lived at Lilla Essingen, the other side of the bridge Västerbron.

I got a job, selling language courses, like a door knocker. Before one had to start trading, one had to learn by heart, everything that one would say to the customer. It was a very psychologically elaborate framework that one could hardly say no to. We worked in large apartment buildings, which in many cases had elevators. Then you would laugh as much as you could in the lift so that you were "happy" when knocking on the doors. And you would knock many times, "knock, knock, knock, knock". I remember once when I knocked on a door, and a woman opened when she saw me, and she was angry, and said, only my children are tapping in that fashion. And then she slammed the door again with a hard bang. We were supposed to "interview" the person who opened the door, and there was no talk of selling. In this interview you asked smart questions to the customer, who finally replied that he would like to learn to speak a new language, and then the order book was taken out, but the pen dropped from the edge of the table so that it lay at the customer's feet, and I did not intend to pick it up, the customer was supposed to pick it up and keep it in their hand. Really psychologically calculated.

I sold well and made money. But my conscience started to feel bad; it didn't feel right to work this way. The customer almost didn't have a chance. And we didn't know the total sales price, and there were added costs which we didn't know anything about. We lost a good friend who bought a language course from me, and she got angry at these additional costs and wanted to cancel the purchase, but I couldn't do anything, the company didn't want to cancel. Unfortunately I was sad about this, and finally, I gave notice and quit.

Employment at Olivetti

I went again to the Employment Service and applied for a job. There they found a vacant sales job at Olivetti! So the customer service woman called the branch manager SG, at Olivetti, and got the answer that they had already filled that position. But SG asked who is looking for a job. Then she told him that I had been working as a door to door salesman selling white goods. Then SG said, send him here, such a man I want to meet, that has been able to support himself by door to door. I came to their office on Kungsgatan 24 and met SG. He said that those who can support themselves on door to door are always welcome as salesmen. I got the job and started selling calculators, typewriters. I had a sales manager called Bo. Then I worked for a while under Bertil, who was the sales manager. Who had started a branch in Södertälje, where I later started as a salesman with a rural district that covered Trosa, Vagnhärad and the southern suburbs of Stockholm. There I also sold other office products. Everything went very well.

I married Irmeli

We married in Trollhättan's church 18th February 1967, because most of my relatives lived there. We moved in after the wedding, to an apartment in Ektorp, Stockholm, we had to pay 5000 kronor "under the table" for the studio, that was also a costly rental. It was four rooms and a kitchen. I had to get an extra job as a newspaper boy and distribute DN- and SvD-papers. To afford the rent, we let out two rooms, to two Italian men. One had a restaurant, and the other had no job. I arranged for him to have a position to deliver newspapers. I first started 5 in the morning, but after a while, I got more jobs, and sometimes I got up at 2 AM at night and worked till 6 AM. After finishing with the papers, I slept a little while before I went to work at Olivetti. But one morning, the Italian man knocked on our bedroom door and said: "Larsong, Larsong, aksidang, aksidang" (Larsson, Larsson, accident, accident). I got up and asked what happened. He went down the hill in Björknäs but got such speed because his brakes had stopped working, he went up to the next hill and was going down the next cliff when he chooses to drive off the road on the hillside. I went there with him and towed the car back.

The sales job went well, and I regularly received a commission. I got several offers from my customers to work for them. I denied every company who was interested in me. But then I was offered by John Forssell AB in Uddevalla to become branch manager in Trollhättan. It was alluring, and I asked Irmeli what she thought, and she said yes.

Moved to Trollhättan 1967

My dad Herman on his moped

Then we moved down to my parents for a few months. Now we had become a family of three, Irmeli had just given birth to our son Robert. We stayed at Svedenborgsgatan 5, on the second floor of my parents during this time. My mother always thought we would come to Trollhättan, she enlisted us in a queue for an apartment for us for several years. We were going to get a new apartment, with two rooms and a kitchen, on Lantmannavägen 40, bottom floor. Rolf, my cousin, transported our furniture to Trollhättan on his truck. And I was ready to start with John Forssell office machines etc. I sold the same products here as I with Olivetti, with the addition of copy machines and Kinnarps office furniture. My district was from the city of Trollhättan, down south to the town of Lilla Edet and up north to the state of Dalsland!

Talked about Australia

In 1968 we started discussing moving to Australia, because I started paying a lot of tax, sometimes it was more than 50% tax. Moving was attractive to us not paying that high tax. Australia advertised its country in Sweden through its consulate in Stockholm. We compared the tax pressure in Sweden, sex and immorality spreading, and we felt it was not the right country for children to grow up in. We also used to go to Spain during the holidays, so we were attracted to living in a warmer climate.

On one of the trips to Spain, we had a frontal collision with a large truck. I drove about 110 km/h, and we collided on a bridge, my car tore up his front tyres, and we slid along his side. My driver's door was very demolished, this was undoubtedly a guardian angel who saved us all from certain death. Irmeli's sister Sirpa, Outi and Tauno were in the grey Saab 95. This happened just north of Perpignan in France. We arrived in Spain the next day. I brought an Olivetti Multisumma20 with me to sell in Spain, although I did not speak the language at all, I managed to sell it, and they paid me for it.

After that holiday we drove all the way from Spain to Sweden. The police in Spain and all the countries just laughed and made gestures for our demolished car. But the Swedish police did not laugh but said that we can only drive directly to our home, and repair the vehicle.

Migration to Australia

Emigration to Australia

We decided in 1969 to apply for emigration to Australia. Everything seemed very interesting. And for a family of three, it would cost 175 kronor. We chose to use, and it wasn't long before we were approved as emigrants. Then I contacted the CEO of Olivetti in Stockholm and asked if he could arrange a sales job for me in Australia. After some time we were told that I was welcome to work with Olivetti in Australia, and would get a car and $60 per week plus commission as a salary. But the employment was dependent on whether I could speak English. (I spoke very poor English).

I submitted my resignation application to Olivetti in Sweden and started making a wooden box during the autumn of 1969, which was about one cubic meter (1x1x1 cubic meter). Where we had our precious possessions, porcelain and the my mothers dining table. Unfortunately, my wife got a miscarriage at Vänersborg's hospital in February 1969. It was, and we mourned. In November 1969, we went to Stockholm where Irmeli's sister Sirpa and her husband Kaj lived, to say goodbye. Sirpa gave birth to a son, Göran. So we had to go to maternity ward and visit her and say goodbye.

Boat trip with MS Achille Lauro

On the 17th of November, we flew to London, and my sales manager, Bertil's daughter Christina was a tour leader. We stayed at a motel in London and went by bus down to Southampton where MS Achille Lauro was waiting to take a lot of other emigrants and us as well!

It was a journey of about four weeks, via the Azores, Sicily, Naples, Genoa, Santa Cruz de Tenerife, Cape Town, Fremantle and finally Melbourne. Now, I had to try to learn English quickly, because I could practically speak no English. It was an Italian boat, and many Italians worked on the ship. The Italians were so excited by our son Robert and wanted to borrow him and invite him to eat ice cream etc. He had blond and curly hair, which was a contrast to the Italian piers on the boat.

The trip continued the next day to Naples, where we also stayed overnight. But Robert and I went into town and ate at a restaurant. Irmeli didn't feel well and stayed on the boat. After the restaurant visit, I asked Robert to stand still outside the restaurant while I filmed him with my Super8 movie camera. But it was boring for Robert to wait while I shot and he ran away. I stopped filming and quickly got caught up with him because I could risk losing him in Naples. Everything went well, and I packed my camera, and we went back to the boat. We continued with the ship to the next port, which was Genoa in northern Italy. Again it was overnight, and with only a short sightseeing tour of the city, the journey continued the next day.

We met three Swedish couples on the boat. I remember Rolf and Eva and another Eva among others. We spent a lot of time on the ship which took 4-5 weeks.

The next port of call was Tenerife in the Canary Islands. There we went ashore in the city of Santa Cruz de Tenerife and ate some squid in a restaurant, afterwards Irmeli's face, and body flared up, with red spots. We went back to the boat and visited the doctor there, who gave her an injection, and she was fine the next day. I had a stomach ache after this restaurant visit and also visited the doctor. My English was very poor. I had only read English one year in school and had almost no opportunity to practice my little English because on the trips to Spain we have to use Spanish a bit because the Spanish speak practically no English at all. I opened my dictionary and checked out a word for pain, found the word "evil" in English. I told the doctor that I had "evil in my stomach"! He seemed to understand and gave me some medicine. Later, I realised that "evil" means such as the devil. Yes, it was not the first mistake in my attempt to speak English; many more were to come.

We continued our journey towards Cape Town in South Africa, when we crossed the equator, the boat had a tradition of holding a special party on board which meant that you would get "baptised" and given a new name. The first passenger would introduce themselves to King Neptune and get a new name from himself. I do not remember my name now. Then his assistants began to dress us in food and eggs etc. all over the body. Then one was led to the large swimming pool to be rinsed off if one did not slip first on the floor of all the food that lay on the boat deck. They had competitions on the boat, where one sat on a log over a smaller pool with a pillow in his hand fighting his opponent with a cushion.

The first one who fell off the trunk and in the pool had lost. The winner who had won all his fights got the first prize.

MS Achille Lauro was a two class ship, with a first class and second class. One could not go to the first class because the doors were locked, and only the staff could unlock the doors. Irmeli and I danced a lot on the boat, to the music band, almost every night. One evening the captain came to us and asked if Irmeli and I would like to go to first class and dance and encourage the older people who were there. We were invited by the captain to eat and drink whatever we wanted. We said yes, and went there the following day. We danced there and sat down at a table with two old English ladies. We talked a lot with them. They asked what I was working with. I said the selling office machines. They looked at me in horror and asked, "How can you get by on that!" How can you cope with such a job? Well, I said, I am doing well. We then became small in their eyes of the lower class. Irmeli and I thought it was boring in the first class. The captain asked us several times if we didn't like to go there another time, but we declined.

We brought Robert sometimes to kindergarten on board, but he didn't like it and cried several times, he did not like to be left alone. He was always with us at home in Sweden, when Irmeli worked, she did it at night when I was home. So it was still one of us at home.

We arrived in Cape Town and went ashore, and took a

guided bus tour around the city with surroundings. We went past the hospital where Christian Barnard was working. He made the first heart transplant in the world. In the city, there were four different toilets, two for white and two for black. The next day we were heading towards Fremantle in Australia. The boat did not go in a straight line, because then it became a long journey because the earth is round, the ship turned a little south which was the shortest road between Cape Town and Fremantle. Here we had to experience the rough sea, it was rocking a lot, but neither Irmeli nor I felt sick. We have never been seasick. Unfortunately, some people did not make the journey but died. Believe that there were six who died, and the bodies had to lie somewhere in a "body bag".

Two weeks after we left Cape Town, we arrived in Fremantle in Western Australia. The first impression I got was that it looked like the Wild West in the USA. I had read a lot about Micky and Salasso in that booklet that came out every week when I was in the school age. And then I had seen these high facades and bars reminiscent of what I just saw in Fremantle. We went into Perth after our passports stamped for the first time in Australia on the 18th of December, 1969. Perth was a beautiful city. We went to Kings Park, which was high and overlooking Perth. We had a picnic lunch, which we all three shared. Robert liked it much.

After the visit to Fremantle, we headed for the final destination Melbourne, Australia. It was just a two-day journey. We arrived and brought our bags with us, but the big box had to wait until we had found an apartment. A bus was waiting for us to take us to Bonegilla, which is just near the border to NSW, outside Wodonga and the vacant military facility with barracks.

The bus stopped first at a kiosk where they had ordered a packed lunch for all travellers. Then it continued to Bonegilla. I sat next to the bus driver in the front, who spoke a rough Australian accent, I got a shock and understood almost nothing at all. I tried to guess what he said and answered either yes or no. It became frustrating because I thought I had just learned a little more English on the boat during these four weeks. Now I had to start over again and learn Australian. Pooh !! The language seemed to come from further down the throat. Example: Mount Isa is pronounced as "Meontoisa"!

Bonegilla

The bus arrived at Bonegilla, and we were delegated to a barrack with two rooms because we had a child. No shower or toilet, only two rooms with beds and a table and chairs. Toilet and shower were in another building. It was the 22nd of December, 1969 and it was about + 40C in the shade! And Christmas was near at hand. I heard the radio playing Bing Crosby's "I am dreaming of a white Christmas"! I got a yearning to go back to the winter. Irmeli was lying in the sun on the lawn sunbathing, but I sat under the tree in the shade. A car with a trailer arrived and handed out Christmas presents to the children. We ate in the canteen. We started to thrive after Christmas and got some Australian friends, who had also been emigrants once upon a time. They were Polish who lived in Wodonga. They asked if we wanted to go on a picnic, yes of course we said. We followed them to a "Fish and Chips-shop" and bought a piece of grilled fish with deep-fried potato chips. Our friends had only purchased the deep-fried potato chips. Everything wrapped up in a newspaper with a white butcher paper separating the food from the black newspaper ink. We sat in the park and ate, and noticed that they only ate the potatoes, we thought it was a little unusual, and could not imagine eating only potatoes. But but.

We learned a little about what was on offer in the furniture stores, and the style was completely different, not really in our taste at all. There was no IKEA at that time. We checked the cars, and the most prominent brands were Ford and Holden. Holden is the same as Opel in Europe but is only produced in Australia and exported to some islands and New Zealand. It was mostly six-cylinder engines they were quite powerful. We liked them — a little American influence instead of European.

Tennis was popular there, and we thought it was interesting, so Irmeli and I went into the sports shop and bought a complete set-up, with clothes racket and balls. We started playing a couple of times. Then, we lost interest, and there was no more playing of tennis. But at least we had a go.

Now it was time for the English lessons at the venue. It was an Australian woman who taught us. I remember the first phrases: "Don't put your shoes on before you put your socks on! Put your socks on before you put your shoes on!"

The train ride to Sydney

The time went by, and I decided to call my employer, Olivetti Australia Pty Ltd in January 1970. I spoke to the Personnel manager Ivan and said we had arrived in Australia, I made an appointment with him at the end of January, to meet him at the office on, 1 Castlereagh Street in Sydney. In the heart of Sydney.

We got a train ticket from Wodonga to Sydney Central Station and started our journey. After several hours we arrived in Sydney. There on the platform were two men in black suits waiting for us. They asked our names and asked us to come along to the big black car, almost like a limousine. They drove us south to a suburb called Matraville, and there was another similar military facility we checked into! This was considerably more central than Bonnegilla, who was out in the bush. We got a double room there too, but no shower or toilet, it was located further down the hall. We enjoyed this seemingly simple environment. Irmeli has always had an incredible ability to make herself at home in all situations and to make it homely. It was vacation time in January. And so my booked visit was at the end of January.

I bought the Sydney Morning Herald newspaper every day, and sat with my Swedish dictionary and read English, but I had to look up almost every word in the newspaper and check in the dictionary what it meant. It was hard, because when I came to the same word again, I had forgotten what it meant, and had to look it up again. Pooh! I had to get my Australian driver's license from the Department of Motor Transport. There was no photo on it, just some text and my signature. It was the best identity you could have in Australia. When I went to the bank they asked for ID, then I showed my Swedish passport, but it was not accepted, nor my Swedish driving license, which both had my photo. Then I showed the Australian driver's licence, and it was accepted.

We made our first visit to one of the RSL (Retired Soldiers League) clubs there, it was a club in memory of the fallen soldiers of the world wars. You could eat, drink, and play on the slot machines there. Irmeli found a slot machine where someone had apparently left it with a lot of money in it. Imagine people just going the slot machine with money in it. But Irmeli thought that this must have been really her happy day because there was a lot of money in the machine. So she started playing. A lady came to her and said it was her machine, she had just sat down to rest and to drink some beer. Irmeli humbly apologised to the lady, and she said, OK, keep the money and continue to play. They invited us to sit at their table, they were very kind to us, and we became good friends.

I continued to learn Australian, and also looked specifically at the news on TV because it was easier to understand because they were closer to the Brittish spoken English. I was training Australian language intensively during the weeks that remained until my appointment with the personnel manager.

Employment at Olivetti Sydney

It was time for me to go into town and meet Ivan, and I was nervous about how it would go. He came out and picked me up in the waiting room, and when I got into his office, I discovered that he had no typewriter. So I sighed with relief within me because if I had demonstrated a typewriter I would have had to talk a lot. We first talked generally, then he asked me to demonstrate his calculator, which was a Divisumma24GT.
I asked him for an A4 sheet of paper and wrote down a list of sums:

12 x 12 = 144
5x5 = 25
6x6 = 36
Total of 205

This type of English is almost the same as Swedish here, i.e. division, multiplication, plus, minus and total. It went well, and he was satisfied, and I got my job confirmed. My first district was in the centre of Sydney. I picked up my car, which was a burgundy Renault 10, this year's (1970) model. I was allowed to use privately also if I only pay for petrol.

The sales office was on Riley Street. I got to work with a sales manager named Michael. He was from England and spoke Oxford English. At the same time, I tried to learn the Australian. When he noticed that I pronounced the words in Australian, he corrected me every time. Then I continued with this mix of languages. Because my language level was so low, I couldn't call customers like any other of the 40 salesmen in the office. My only chance was to go out in the town with a machine under my arm. Now there were smaller calculators such as Multisumma20 that were new on the market. I knew the whole product range from Sweden, so it was easy. The machines I knew inside out. It was just the language that was the Achilles heel for me. I had about one kilometre to walk to the city, and I took the little Multisumma20 with me under my arm. Went up in these multi-storey office buildings and stood there knocking on the first door, with nervousness and at the same time excitement. The door was opened, and I presented myself as Curt Larsson from Olivetti and gave them my business card. I said in very broken English: "Me show you this machine"? (I thank God that the Australian always wants to give someone a fair go, and is also friendly towards immigrants.

Especially from Northern Europe.) The answer was Yes, welcome. I usually asked for an A4 sheet of paper. I demonstrated the three different counting methods on Multisumma20, because it did not have the division function. After the demonstration, I offered them to keep the machine on a demo for a few days. Sometimes the answer was yes, and sometimes no thanks. When I had left the machine for demonstration, I had to go down to the office and pick up a new machine from the man from Switzerland, Charles at the warehouse. He also had language problems, but it was possible to communicate with him.

Back to the city again with another new machine. Sometimes when I got to the office, which was a large room with many sales associates without partitions, like an office landscape, the phone rang on some desk. The salesmen said that's your call, Curt. I said no, I can not take the call, with the result that no salesman answered, and I felt very needy to answer. Oh what a hassle, because most conversations were really in rough Australian, I had big problems to understand. Asked the customer to repeat what he said, and if I didn't understand, I asked him to spell. It was very awkward. Imagine that you are interested in buying something and the salesman asks you finally to spell instead of to speak. I think no one hangs up on me, thank God for that! The other salespeople sat mostly at their desks and rarely carried out machines the way I did. They were able to communicate and build up a customer base, and sold the machines, or made appointments on the phone. I listened when the salesmen, talked to customers on the phone.

You have to start and leave impressions on the customers that you talk with, and show them that you are a little more sophisticated in terms of language and pronunciation. The word I heard was "super seeded". I liked the word "super" because it meant big or grand, you know that there are supermarkets, where you can buy all kinds of food. I thought that "seeded", meant pages (Swedish sidor, pronounced "seedor"). So I guessed this word "superseded meant "versatile" "great-looking". I was waiting for the next customer to call in so that I could impress him a little with my new found knowledge in the English language. It wasn't long before a customer called and was interested in buying a calculator. But this new Multisumma20 was a brand new product on the market, and that was the one I liked to sell. Then other calculators would be discontinued. They were thus outdated. But now to this customer that I had on the handset, I told him that we had a completely new machine that had come out on the market and it was "superseded". The customer did not comment and gave no particular response, to my surprise. Don't remember if he bought anything at all. But what did the word "super seeded" mean? Well that means "replaced, something newer has come, old model, left". I actually said that this brand new machine on the market had been replaced. It was an old model... It was just the opposite of what I wanted to say. The guys in the office got a good laugh at my newly acquired status in the English language.

But I had to continue to knock on doors, to look for new customers.
In March, we had a sales competition, so that all 40 salesmen would be motivated. There was also a small price for those who won the. I worked and sweating on. Remember that it was high summer with very high temperatures, which could be + 40C or more. So it was both physical and mental sweating. I had many machines out on demonstration, but I always came back the next day after to see how the customer liked it, and if they understood the functions of the machines.
But then came the next test for me. A customer was interested in an electric typewriter, and they weighed between 22 kilograms and 27 kilos. I picked up a typewriter and started walking one kilometre to the

centre. There were buses, but it was almost more challenging to go by bus. I decided to walk to town. Rather than to stand on the bus holding the typewriter with one hand, and the other hand the pole. So the best thing was to walk. The typewriter cut into the waist, so you had to stop several times and change between the left and right waist. Now it was April, and I was second place among 40 salesmen. It gave me a lot of courage and satisfaction.

One day Irmeli was out and walking with Robert around where we lived, then Robert got to see something interesting on the footpath, and picked it up it looked like a black stick. But it turned out to be a poisonous snake. Irmeli was quick and took the snake from Robert and would throw it away, but she dropped it, and it fell on her ankle and bite her. An Australian man passed by, who quickly identified the snake, and took off his belt, which he tied around her leg. He stopped a taxi, and they promptly went to the emergency room, where Irmeli received an injection. Irmeli felt sick, but they arrived on time, so there were no complications!

Moving to our first apartment

We had now found a one bedroom apartment, living room combined with kitchen, on 1 Keith Street in Dulwich Hill. We had bought a double bed on wheels and chairs and a sofa as well as TV. Once when we laid down in bed, we almost rolled out through the window. The window was lower than the bed. But fortunately, the bed stopped right at the window pane. It was parquet flooring, so if you were not careful when lying down, you could fly out through the window. We lived on the first floor.

Then it was time to call the transport company and get our precious possessions from Sweden in the wooden box that I had constructed. The carrier came with a truck, but they had no lift or ramp, so they pushed off the box, then a big crash was heard. It turned out that our Höganäs ceramic service had gone into a thousand pieces. No replacement for the transport company. Only bad luck.

Robert had started to go to pre-school now. And Irmeli got a part-time job as an inspector at ICI, a company that made glass measurements that were used in the hospitals and laboratories, the grading of millilitres was critical, and Irmeli who was a trained nurse was very meticulous.

During the major holidays we went out with the company car, in January 1971 on my first holiday we went to Mount Kosciuszko which was 2,228 metres above sea level, that is Australia's highest peak. Irmeli had then given birth to our daughter Camilla, 12.11.1970, so she was only a couple of months old. But the sun was intense, and Camilla got a little sunburnt, but we covered her face with sunscreen. We continued this trip out in the Australian bush, and Camilla needed food quite often, which meant that we had to stop occasionally and give her food. Once, it was in an area that looked like a desert, far away from urban areas. Then suddenly, a car stopped; first, we got a little scared and wondered what they wanted. But the driver winded down his window and asked if we were OK. I said, no problem, everything is OK. Then he just went on. It seems to be customary to stop and ask if anyone has stayed in the wilderness, because it can be a problem, or if you are without water etc. Much can happen in the desert.

Facing a shotgun

We bought a new Ford Falcon Station wagon with a six-cylinder petrol engine. It was a popular car in Australia. I had returned my company car. I got petrol money instead when I was working. There was a lot of training for the salesmen at Olivetti. The first training conference I had to go to was in Adelaide. I had to choose to fly there or take the car. Then I asked Irmeli if she wanted to come with me to Adelaide, and she certainly wanted to. So I told the boss I was driving to Adelaide.

We packed the bags and went to Adelaide via Dubbo, Nyngan, Cobar, Broken Hill, which was the long road 1660 kilometres, through desolate hills. We were going to stay in Cobar, a journey of about 8 hours from Sydney. We stopped to enjoy a milk bar (it is a small, simple restaurant), in Trangie, which is a desolate little village between Dubbo and Nyngan. It was late afternoon, we ordered our coffee and waited for it to be finished. There was a man there who looked with a weird look at us. I felt awkward in some way. But we forgot it and finished our coffee and continued our journey towards Nyngan. The roads out in the bush are

usually very straightforward, as there are not many hills or mountains in the forest, especially in NSW. Then I saw in the rearview mirror that a Holden Monaro approached us quite quickly, it's Holden's fastest car, with a powerful V8 engine. When he came parallel with me, he slowed down, and he picked up a shotgun and aimed at us. I pushed the gas accelerator pedal in the bottom and drove away from him, but deep down, I knew I wouldn't have a chance with his big V8 engine. Soon he caught up with us, but now I had no hesitation, I slammed the breaks and quickly turned back in the direction of Trangie. But the Monaro did not give up but caught up with me again, and this time I again turned around again, but against Nyngan, this time I drove slower, not to drive too far away from Trangie. After a while he caught up with me, and then I turned again, but now I drove into Trangie, and directly to the police, it was late in the evening now, and we knocked on the police door. The police opened, and we quickly explained that we had been chased by a fool on the road who threatened us with a shotgun. Then the police said, "Don't come here and make trouble"!
We looked for a motel and checked in, the next day it was quiet, so we went on to Adelaide. We then went back to the conference without any further complications.

We also bought a block of land in Greystanes for $5000, which would be an investment and the idea was to build our first house there. We paid off on this block of land every month.

In Sydney, my sales continued, with good results, I

normally would be amongst the top three salesmen. The salesmen were from a mix of different European countries. We had an accountant born in Holland and came to Australia after finishing his school in Holland he was now in his fifties, and kept track of the economy and all orders. He spoke perfect English. I heard him count audibly once in Dutch and was surprised. I asked him why he counted in Dutch and said he had never practised headcount in any other language, and if he were to count in English, it would just be wrong.

My wife was partly at home with the children when the kids came home from school, but she also worked. Once she was out shopping and went to the fruit dealer and wanted to buy apples that were ready to eat. But she wanted ripe apples, not the greens. To make sure, she asked for "raped apples", the fruit dealer looked at her very surprised because of course, he had no raped apples, so he asked her "are you pulling my leg". Irmeli felt very offended and thought that he was vulgar to a woman who tried to communicate to him, she said: "I am not pulling your leg, you dirty old man". The word rape and ripe sounds almost equally pronounced, and Irmeli made a mistake in the pronunciation and thereby entered a conflict.

One day I was going to lay down our daughter Camilla in the cot when I saw something black in her cot, on the white sheet. I held Camilla in my arms and laid her on our bed next to her bed. I looked a little more at this little black thing, but couldn't decide what it was. I went to the kitchen and picked up an empty glass jar, and quickly put it over this black thing. Then I saw that it was a spider. I took the glass jar to the pharmacy to identify it. They said it was a funnel web spider, by far the most dangerous spider in the world. It had rained a lot, and we lived on the 2nd floor of 107 Livingstone road in Marrickville. In this humid weather, the spiders creep up higher and look for a dry place. It had entered through an open window and to the bed on the opposite side of the room. Camilla was then less than a year old.

Thoughts of returning to Sweden

We started to compare a little how you lived in Australia versus in Sweden. It was freezing inside the apartment in the winter in Australia. One must have radiators standing on the floor in all rooms so as not to freeze. But in the toilet, there was no room for any radiator, so it was freezing cold there. In the bathroom, there was a strip heater over the wash basin, and this strip heater radiated the heat downwards when standing and washing. But the heat was so nasty dry and warm, not comfortable. There were no garbage drops in the stairways of the flats, but one had to go out to the yard and put all their garbage in your bin 50-litre barrel, which had a lid. When it was time for refuse collection, a truck with an open back came. A man trampled down the garbage, and the other men emptied garbage bins up and down. Sometimes there was a wind that blew away some trash over the neighbourhood. It also smelled. The contrast was that in Sweden comes a big truck with a container, that opens up in the rear, the workers are fetching the 300 litres bins at each house, using a hand trolley, a crane in the back of the truck empties this bin into the container. Then the rear end closes up.

The mail was delivered in a small metal mailbox by the street, they were so tiny that only half of the large business envelopes got inside, and the other half was out in the weather, and if it rained, it got wet.

We use to read Swedish newspapers at the Norwegian Seamen's Church in Sydney, where we saw ads on food and noticed that some prices were lower than in Australia. What we didn't realise was that this was special prices and not regular prices. So really we compared Swedish special prices with regular prices in Australia.

We moved to Windsor road in Dulwich Hill before returning to Sweden. We rented a flat of Jenny and Dennis, who had a villa with three apartments in. Jenny and Dennis were Turks and were very friendly to us. All of a sudden, we discovered food was inside our door when we got home from being out. She made some delicious food. Dennis had a weakness for other girls, he travelled to England, but we didn't know what he was doing there. There were many children there for Robert and Camilla to play with. Once, a girl hit Robert in the head with a bottle. The bottle didn't break, but Robert cried. When Camilla or Robert had a birthday, they had a big children's party.
Irmeli was always very good and did fine with all kinds of decorations, and of course, we had a great birthday cake. But as a rule, we bought it from a baker who was Greek or Italian, because we could not find this kind of cake among the Australian bakeries. Our favourite cake was Black Forrest cake, but there was no connection whatsoever to Swartzwald's cake, only the name was

shared. It was a cake with cream and cherry decorations .... yum...yum! We sometimes amused ourselves by going to watch World Championship Wrestling. After all, it's a show, a wrestling match where everything seems to be allowed. They have blood vials in their hands when they fight, so it looks like they are bleeding. But accidents happen, and sometimes severe accidents. They dress up like monsters sometimes! One group is a good one, and another group is the evil one. After a while, we had enough.

On the weekends we travelled out into the country and looked at attractions and mostly just out in nature and had meat to grill with us. There were usually barbecue areas along the roads throughout Australia.

Places we liked in NSW were:

Big Banana in Coffs Harbor, on the north coast towards Brisbane it was a banana plantation, with a small train that went out into the estate, and a restaurant where you could drink coffee.

Berrima south of Sydney, a historic village with an old prison, and a lot of nostalgia.

Sofala is near Bathurst, where you can try to pan for gold. We found a transparent glass stone that delighted us. We thought that we something of value, we checked the value. Irmeli and I were very happy to have received this treasure. And we were ready to sell it, wondering just about the hundreds of dollars we could get. There were "experts" on the location who could give us an appreciation of the value. We went to one of them and presented our findings. He received it and looked carefully at it. Then came his score; we listened with excitement. He said it was a piece of a green glass bottle. Guess how disappointed we were, who thought we would strike it rich.

Lighting Ridge, opal field, is located in the northern part of NSW in the middle of the border to Queensland north of Dubbo and straight up to the border of Queensland. We went there once to experience opal mining. No one says anything about what they have found. We went into the pub, there are pubs almost everywhere, and this was no exception. There was a wild west feeling. No one talks about their findings. It can be of significant sums in the values for opals. Some are making a living there. Everyone walks around, looking to the ground to discover something that glitters too. But you have to wash with water and wash the clay and then gently sift the gravel with your hands. You can register a claim, by paying a small amount, you can do this in many places in Australia if you want to dig for gold, sapphires and opals etc. Then you can start digging there. But others just walked around looking on the ground. One day it had rained pretty much after we had been there, but we heard about it. A lady went there and was looking and seeing something black glittering. She picked up this shiny black stone, it seemed fine, she went and got it valued, and it was a black opal that was worth about $4000, which was a considerable amount of money in that year.

White Cliffs, NSW, is located just before reaching Broken Hill on the South Australia border. It is an old place where there have been many excavations for opals. Some large areas have become places of residence after it has been emptied of gems. Many people live there, it has natural air conditioning, because the temperature is quite constant inside a cave. You do not need heat or cold. There is at least one hotel there, and we have stayed there, the rooms are cosy with the reddish stone walls. They have drawn electricity and furnished nicely. It is to recommend for anyone who wants to stay a little more comfortable when looking for opals. Once we were in a hotel, which was also a pub, in the nearest town, Wilcannia. There are many Aborigines there. When we went down to the pub to have breakfast, we sat down at the bar as so many others did. The innkeeper behind the bar had a revolver in his pocket, we were told by him because there could arise a quarrel or fuss between the guests, and he wanted to be sure he would keep his life and defend himself. He whispered to us that we were sitting on the wrong side of the bar, he said it was the black side, and we did best to move to the other side. The police had fled the city, due to that it was a significant security risk to be there.

We met Alf and Lyn there, Alf had a small farm outside the town on the way to Cobar. They invited us to come to them which we accepted. Our children Robert and Camilla were with us, and they had four children so that they could play together. We went there and got to experience an Australian farmhouse for the first time. All the animals were out, and there was no barn. They had sheep and used sheepdogs to move the sheep. Alf went on his 250cc motorcycle with the dog standing on the tank between his legs. And how this dog could stay on the tank is a mystery, as he drove over large tufts and sometimes jumped with the motorcycle. The dogs got nothing to eat in the morning, and they only drank water. They worked unabated all day in the heat, which could go up to + 40C, they ran a lot back and forth and listened to his commands. The dogs were excellent. Late in the afternoon, it was time to go home and have dinner leaving the sheep in the fields. The dogs then got a big meal before it was time for them to rest. The next morning they barked, and wanted to go out again and run, they loved it!

We became good friends with them and continued to visit them. There was a runway for a twin-engine aircraft near, and it is used for the flying doctors. But even a priest is also using it for sharing the message of Jesus with people.

On the way home, I remembered a colleague from Olivetti, who was from the bush. He told me that they have a large butchery in the outback. He worked there once, and he saw a rat running between the meat and ending up in the meat grinder. He reported this to his boss, but he replied that they would add some more spices to the sausage. Their sausage is perfect for BBQ. It resembles the Swedish pork sausage.
Later we come to Bathurst. You can also look at the old prison with some exciting stories that the guides are telling almost every day. There they also compete with cars in the Grand Prix. But we did not watch live on

this but watched it on TV when the races were broadcast.

Katoomba in Blue Mountain just west of Sydney, we occasionally went to watch the "Three Sisters", there are three rock formations, at a mountain cliff in Katoomba.

Gulgong or the so-called Ten dollar town portrayed on the old 10 dollar bill, located north of Mudgee, north of Lithgow and Katoomba. This is a very picturesque city, where you can experience a bit of the past in Australia. But there are many other cities with a strong historical origin. Too many to repeat.

Snowy Mountains is a popular ski resort with ski lifts in the winter between June and August. You can rent ski equipment, and it is about 7 hours drive from Sydney a straight run south towards the Victorian border.

Canberra is on the road to Snowy Mountain and is a very modern city from 1913 with now about 380,000 inhabitants. (2017) There are a large parliament house and large museums etc.
Nowadays, the highway goes all the way from Sydney to Canberra and also to Melbourne. But at our time it was a mostly paved road. And sometimes gravel road in the bush. This has now disappeared, and in general, there are paved roads around the country.
On Australia's east coast, it is usually beautiful sandy beaches,

Sydney is primarily known for its sandy beaches, but

you have to be very careful, and preferably not swim alone. The sharks come in, and you have lifeguards who put out the red flags, and you have to bathe inside these flags so that they keep checking on all bathers. Sometimes there will also be strong undercurrents that can pull people far out under the sea surface, and someone has drowned because of this. Even if you are a skilled swimmer, it may not help you. Be also careful not to swim where there is a warning for "Box Jelly Fish" (a type of jellyfish) it has up to 10 metres long tentacles and if you are hit by them, and then it can become a painful death. The light blue "Blue Ring Octopus" also exists on the beach sometimes among rocks. It is stunning but deadly toxic. Sometimes children have played with it, but it is hazardous.

We had another sales competition at Olivetti, with a trip to Hayman Island as a prize. Everyone who had reached a certain level of sales won the trip plus a week's pay. At the end of 1971, I found out that I had won this trip. But I declined because all of our comparisons had led us to decide to go back to Sweden. We sold our block of land in Greystanes and made a profit of about $5000. Which we could use to pay for the trip to Sweden.

Migrating back to Sweden

Going back to Sweden

I contacted John Forssell AB in Uddevalla and asked if I could get the job back, and I got it. Mum had queued for an apartment at Eidars which we reached at Lantmannavägen 12 in Trollhättan. Everything was ready. We ordered a boat trip with Australis, which was the world's largest one-class liner. No first class. We went from Sydney Harbour on January 3, 1972, and first stayed at Suva in Fiji. There we went ashore and got to see a native village with dance and singing. This time we were a family of four.

The next stop was Acapulco in Mexico, where the boat could not go into port but had to lie outside and a boat picked us up so we could see the Indians, who were Aztec's, to dive from a 41 metres high cliff into the shallow sea. It takes years of training before divers are ready to take on the dangerous cliffs of La Quebrada. Most begin at five or six, and divers join the show at 15. They dive six days a week – rain or shine – and an average of ten dives per day. After swimming across the narrow, 4 metres wide channel, the young men climb with bare hands and feet to a platform about 40 metres above the sea level. There, they pray for protection at the altar of the Virgin of Guadalupe before making their leap and dive. Timing is critical for the divers. Water depth in the gulch can vary from two to five metres, with an average depth of 4 metres, so divers must time their leap to coincide with the incoming waves.
Then it was time to go through the Panama Canal, but

first overnight in Cristobal. We saw Kungsholm lying there, Irmeli's brother Tommi used to work on that boat, as an entertainer. There we took a taxi to a casino, in the cab there was a little round hole in the window, I asked the taxi driver what it was, he replied that it was a bullet hole. Scary!! At the casino, we change to chips, but the smallest denomination was the US $10. We changed in two chips but no profit.

The next day there was a cruise through the Panama Canal, and then it was set up on deck with buffet lunch. So we could enjoy the beautiful scenery on both sides of the boat. We got to see these locomotives that pulled the boat through all the locks, on both sides.

Then we went to Port Jackson, Florida. We hired a car and went into Miami. We went around a little and looked, especially at Miami beach. There appeared a man and said to Irmeli, that it was important for Camilla to have sun cream on her face. She was just a little over a year old then. Finally, we came to Bremerhaven in Germany, where our trip ended. It was cold, and we bought warm clothes for the kids.

Then we took the train up to Stockholm, where I bought a new suit at Tempo. Then we were ready to visit the in-laws Tauno and Outi Kinnunen in Västerås, on Bangatan 19. It was the first winter for Camilla, but she seemed to like it and fed the ducks along with Robert and Outi, her grandmother. After a few days, it was time to go to Trollhättan and visit grandmother and grandfather, where we would stay a few days until the apartment at Lantmannavägen 12 became available.

But we didn't get a good start here in Sweden but understood why we had moved to Australia and planned to move back again.

For the time being, I worked at John Forssell AB in Trollhättan. We were out in nature a lot, and when spring and summer arrived, we picked berries of all kinds, and mushrooms that we ate as often as we could, to save money for the return trip. I contacted Michael at Olivetti in Sydney and asked if I could come back and work for them. He said I was very welcome! It was lucky for us. We booked the return trip with Fairstar which would go via the Panama Canal and Tahiti and New Zealand. The journey would begin in September 1972 just before the Munich Olympics.

Return to Australia

We went to Rotterdam where Fairstar waited. The first stop was in Southampton, England. It had to stop for regular service of the ship, so we hired a car and travelled to London, where we visited a couple we knew, who had moved back to England from Australia. We stayed with them for a couple of nights, and it was already getting cold and humid weather. We went to see Madam Tussauds and the crown jewels, among other things.

On this trip, we met a Finnish couple named Trevor and Birgitta Majoinen who was going back to Australia. We started partying and spending a lot of time with them on the boat. Sometimes we were up till early in the morning and slept until late in the afternoon. We got a bit up and down with our routines. They became terrific friends with us.

The next stop was the Azores, where Irmeli did not feel right, so it was Robert and me who went into the city. The fruit merchants were delighted in Robert because he had curly and blond hair and stuffed his pockets full of apples.

Next was Curacao in the Caribbean Sea just off Bilbao. There we met an African family who had an old American car, and they drove us around for a while. The houses in the city were in different colours because the mayor got a headache of seeing all the houses in white colours.

Then there was a stop in Bilbao which is at the opening of the Panama Canal, with Cristobal at the other end. Now we started to cruise through the Panama Canal for the second time. It was relaxing as before, there were several swimming poles up on the deck for us and the kids to swim in. The food on the boat was of good class, and the waiters did an excellent job, we enjoyed the trip.

The next port of call was Tahiti, where the boat was received by a dance group who danced on the quay before we could go ashore. After that, we went ashore. We went for a guided tour and then it was time to embark again. The next stop was the second last at Wellington New Zealand. It was our first visit to the island. Fairstar was met by a fireboat that sprayed water from its water cannons straight up into the air to create a rainbow in the light of the clear blue sky. As usual, we took a guided tour, as you usually get a good overview of the place. We got to learn how the native people greet each other, sticking out their tongue. The knife is laid down at the feet, which is the sign of friendship without fights and enmity. They also danced for us, with shouts and grimaces. They do this to deter people from attacking them, and to coerce respect. We continued to the ultimate, Sydney Harbour!

Moving to Killara

There was my boss Michel and waited and waved. He had arranged a villa in Killara in northern Sydney, a prestigious area where only "fine people" lived, such as business executives, captains, etc.

The job was arranged and a car. I started working after a couple of days, and we signed the rental agreement on the villa first.

I asked the CEO if I could not get any compensation for the trip that I won to Hayman Island before I went to Sweden, but he said no, and then he changed his mind so that I got a week's extra payment!
The trip to and from Sweden made a deep hole in our finances. The profit from the sale of our block of land in Greystaynes was almost entirely used up.

The children started attending school in the neighbourhood, and Christmas was approaching. Then the school invited all parents on a "bring a plate" for an event where the children would perform, and everyone would be amused. We went there with our neighbour, who also had children there, attending the same school and grade. We sat at the same table. When the time had come to eat, our neighbour asked where we had our plates. We said, wait a moment we have them in the car. So we came back with our two dishes. They looked a little surprising on our empty plates and said we were expected to have something on the plates. We were surprised, but they said they don't worry share with us. Another neighbour invited us to New Year's celebration in 1972/73, and this was in the upper class with friendly people. But as the alcohol went in, the wisdom disappeared. We just sipped drank juice ourselves, while the others divulge and drank a lot. I do not want to go into what they did, but we were embarrassed and went back home.

Trevor and Birgitta are visiting.

Once at the end of 1972, our Finnish friends called Trevor and Birgitta said they would come to Sydney. They lived in Canberra, and it was about 300 km to Sydney. Then I told Trevor that I had to go and buy Koskenkorva, which is a Finnish alternative for vodka. I didn't like Koskenkorva at all, but since he was a Finn, it was just a friendly gesture from my side. After this visit, there were many visits in the future. We had a very good fellowship with them and became terrific friends.

Olivetti always had a great Christmas party for employees with their families, and it was a party with a Christmas gift and good fellowship. It was much appreciated by all children and a sweet ending to the year.

Moving to Harbord

We started looking for somewhere else to stay. And we were looking for "units", flats that you buy. We went out to the coast and were watching. We didn't have much money now and had to choose the cheapest. We saw a two bedroom apartment with living room and separate kitchen, in Harbord, in Sweden you call it a three-room flat. It cost $19500 we had a down payment of $1000. We got a loan for over 25 years, which we could afford.

This apartment was on Evans Street in Harbord. There was a famous Diggers Leagues Club there, which people used to go to eat, drink and play at the slot machines. At 9 PM, everything was interrupted, and a trumpet fanfare was played, all stood up in salute and silent. It became a silent minute for the dead soldiers.

We had no furniture, only my mother's dining table from Sweden. We used the suitcase as a dining table because we had a lot of things on the dining table. We slept on the carpet on the concrete floor, it was tough to sleep there, but we got used to it after a while. We had decided not to buy something on instalment, and we had to wait until we could afford it. When we were in Sydney city centre, we went to Waltons where they sold furniture and looked, and they had a special offer where you could buy without interest and split the payment into three months. Then we purchased beds for the kids and us. I had built a wardrobe in our bedroom, so there we could hang our clothes. When we got our beds, we got a sore back of sleeping in them, we were so used to the hard concrete floor, and we had to get used to again to the soft beds, after a few weeks it was ok to sleep in the new beds.

We had friends who were police officers and used to go to their party sometimes. But sometimes they used alcohol and drugs. We never tried drugs, one of the wives growing marijuana at home. Once the drink was finished, and one of the police took the car to buy some more alcohol. I asked him, what if a police officer stopped us, he said he was only needed to show his police badge, so that would not be a problem. Fortunately, we were not stopped by the police. Once my wife had taken a little too much liquor when she went to the shopping centre, then the police came, but she started running for some reason, and the police also started to run after her, while she shouted for help: "police, police". Police caught her and said, "We're the police." She hadn't done anything, so they released her at once.

Irmeli with Danny Boy

I wanted to surprise Irmeli with a dog on the birthday of July 29, 1975, so I went to Liverpool where there was a dog breeder, I found a cocker spaniel male puppy, it was the owner's favourite, which she always liked to cuddle. I bought the puppy called Danny Boy and placed him in a large cardboard box. When I arrived, I put the box in front of the door and knocked on the door and ran away. Irmeli came up and opened the door but did not see the carton with the dog in, on the floor, so I knocked once more on the door and ran away. This time she saw the dog when she opened the door, he sat in the box with a blue ribbon around his neck, trembling in fear. But Irmeli's heart melted when she saw the dog. I took the box with me and went inside. Irmeli tucked the puppy under her arm when she worked in the kitchen. She fell in love with the dog. Not to mention the kids, now they had a dog to play with, and to take out.

Trevor and Birgitta visit again.

Trevor called us again, so I said that I had to go and purchase Koskenkorva, so they are welcome. Then it turned silent in the phone, after a short silence, Trevor said, "I am a Christian now, and I do not drink that any more". I didn't first know what to say, but I thought it was not so important to drink alcohol, and also good to not have to drink Koskenkorva, and that wouldn't separate us. So I said, "It doesn't matter, you are welcome anyway". I should ask him what had changed his life. When they arrived, they had parked their blue Ford Falcon down the road, and went up to our apartment and knocked on the door.

It was exciting this time when they came, and there were many questions I had. We spoke English because Trevor did not speak Swedish. For every question I had about his faith, he replied with what the Bible said. Yes, there was the answer, but then I had a new question, it became a discussion, and then he showed me what it said in the Bible about that very thing. After many hours it was time for them to go. We followed down to their car, which we hadn't seen before. They had Christian stickers all over the back of the car with words like Jesus, and Bible words. When we saw these stickers, we were incredibly ashamed and wondered what the neighbours would say. We were happy that the car disappeared, so no one saw us with them.

Despite this, we continued to share fellowship with Trevor and Birgitta for the next six years. And each time we had the same discussions about the Bible and

Jesus, but we kept a low profile, and did not show where we stood in our faith, it was extremely private.

Holidays in Bali

I had won a sales trip to Bali with other colleagues who also qualified. It was a trip for two people, so my wife could come along.

We knew a Danish couple who would look after our children during the week we were living in Bali. We stayed at the Hilton Hotel, and it was a luxurious hotel, all the food, etc. was provided. Also, an optional dinner for two people where you could eat just what you wanted completely free. We booked for this dinner, where we ate the most expensive on the menu a three course with everything included Afterwards, our waiter told us that our dinner cost him the same as his annual salary. They were very poor on the island.

I had trouble connecting the cord to my shaver in the socket and needed a screwdriver to replace the plug. I called on the phone and ordered a "screwdriver". A moment later, a waiter knocked on our door with a tray and a glass on it with an orange colour drink. He said, "screwdriver, sir"! I said, "no, I want screwdriver". He did not understand first, so I showed him what I wanted to do in the room. He then said, "Obeng", which was screwdriver in his language.

We also hired a motorcycle that we both could sit on. We went out into the country, where there were small gravel and clay paths that we rode on. I saw that the roadway changed colour in front of us; it looked like some yellow stuff. When I slowed down, and to my horror, there was chaff across the road. Irmeli jumped off, and I drove gently forward, when the motorcycle suddenly sank into the river, with not much water, it was rocky, so I had to speed up in order not to get stuck in the middle of the river. Finally, over on the other side, Irmeli sat in the back again.

We were going to the mother temple but needed help with which way we should go, in the village in front of us. We stopped there and asked a woman who just had a skirt on her, and bare breasts and a sucking child in her arms. We asked her about the road, but at the same time, we didn't know where to look when the bare-breasted woman spoke to us. It felt so uncomfortable and unusual for us. But she gave us the direction we were going to go, we continued.

The hotel had given us a packed lunch, and the time was right when we were having lunch. We stayed out in the woods, where there were no people. We sat down and began to eat when one after another came out of the woods and stood a few metres away and just looked at us. We greeted them, but could not speak the language, and we continued to the high volcano which was pouring out smoke.

There was a lake in front of the volcano, and we hired a boat with one that rowed us over on the other side. There they showed us a burial ground. There were no graves, and only skeletal heads lined up on the rocks. The guide showed us his relatives with joy, they were not sad but had a belief that "they were fine now". It was getting late in the afternoon, and it would take time to go back, we were offered to go by motorboat back, at a high price. But what could we do, we just paid the price and went back by the speedboat over the lake. What they didn't tell us was that paint was new, and when we sat down in the boat, we got paint on us.

Before we got to the hotel, we went to Kuta beach. People were not shy at all, and they did "all their needs" on the beach one after the other, you could see everything when driving past them. We drove past a man carrying a ready-made table with a burning candle over his head. It was a funeral party with noise and shouts, where also the coffin was carried high over their heads.

Robert, Danny Boy, Camilla

Back in Sydney, Irmeli found Camilla near the cliff playing, then Irmeli became furious and rebuked the Danish couple. Otherwise, the children were Ok.

Irmeli's parents emigrate.

Irmeli's parents emigrated to Australia in May 1975. Tauno had emphysema due to the lacquer used at Asea, the industry he worked for, which had destroyed his lungs and affected the breathing just as if it had been asthma. The doctor said a dry and sunny climate would be suitable for him, which later turned out to be true. We met them at Sydney airport, with our two children. Robert was then almost eight years old, and Camilla was about five years. The children spoke Swedish because I had told the children that we would always talk Swedish at home. We talked to Outi and Tauno, while Camilla was quiet, then Camilla said: "I can also speak English".

They got to stay with us in Harbord for the first time until they had been able to get an apartment, which didn't take long. Their baggage came separately by boat. They moved into a one bedroom apartment with separate living room and separate kitchen, on the third floor on the street next door in Harbord. Tauno said that it was summer and Sunday all the time. He was a pensioner.

Vacation in Queensland

We hired a caravan for our holiday trip to Queensland, and drove with our Ford Falcon station wagon and connected the trailer. It was an exciting journey. We went north from Sydney towards Brisbane, but first, we stayed at Coffs Harbour on the Big Banana Plantation. There we went for a mini train that went through the plantation with a guide. Then we went on to the Gold Coast, where there are many fun places for children to experience. The trip then went through Brisbane, towards Hervey Bay where there are wild horses called Brumby, and there are also dingos. If you are lucky, there are whales there as well. We went up to Rockhampton and Great Keppel Island. There is an underwater observatory, and you can see the small fish in the morning, which is fed by a diver. One can take a photo of them through the glass. Then you can enjoy the beach and eat a sumptuous meal at the five-star restaurant.

Our caravan in flood

We then went south to Mount Morgan, where they had a gold mine that is not in progress but used as a tourist attraction. A very motivated tourist guide made this trip to pleasure. We went on to Emerald, we always stayed at campsites with the caravan, the same here in Emerald, with the exception that there were a lot of light green frogs in the shower. Irmeli didn't want to shower there, only me and the kids. She said they were so disgusting. We went further west to Barcaldine and then straight south to Charlieville. We continue from there to the east to the neighbourhood around Mitchell. There it started to rain, and the rain increased in intensity as well. There was a lot of water on the road, and suddenly the car stopped. I got some moist on the distributor; I stepped out and dried the breaking tips. After a few attempts to start the car, it started but coughed and stopped again after a few metres. I opened the door and noticed that the water just entered the car, so I closed the door quickly. The whole vehicle was partly submerged. And all the traffic had stopped in both directions. I winded down the window and stepped out through the window. People flocked to and were willing to help us. I asked someone if we could cut the wire fence, to use as the towing line. And we did. Irmeli was worried by all the twigs and branches flowing towards, and under the caravan, we started pulling off as many as we could, but many more came, it was hopeless to get rid of them all. Now the steel wire was connected to the car, so I sat in the car and waited for the vehicle, which was about 10-15 metres in front to start driving. But it just jerked, and the line broke off. I went out in front of the car to a place where the line would be half a meter submerged, and the water was up to my knees. I took a step to the right but quickly noticed that I had no foothold, and as a consequence, I fell into the water, which was so deep there that I had to swim back. But I couldn't, I just floated backwards. Then I saw a small green twig stick up, which was the top of a small bush. I figured out at what angle I had to swim to get to this pitiful green bush stalk. I managed to get hold of the branch, while I was facing our car, but it just broke off, then I got hold of the next twig that broke off and then the next twig. Further afield there was a barbed wire fence. I thought if I ended up there, I could drown.

Meanwhile, Irmeli and the others stood and just watched. Irmeli heard a voice behind her that said "freeze", the man came and snatched the end of the black snake that had crept up on her back, and began to swing it around to release it so that it was flung far away finally. There was a jackaroo next to Irmeli with his lasso rope. Irmeli gave him a command that the jackaroo would throw the line to me. He was very accurate, and the rope came with a fantastic speed against me. I raised my arm in the air, and the line flew around me a couple of times. I got hold of it and disappeared under the water while they pulled me up on the road again.

I still had my sunglasses on me, and the sun hat when I got back up on the way again. There was a lot of traffic that had banked up behind us, but no car passed us, for stood in deep water. I checked if there was water in the caravan, but it was still dry. I thought I had to get hold of a truck that could tow us. I started walking behind our car and came to the first truck, and I asked the driver if he could help me. He said "no chance". The water had become too deep, and he didn't want to risk getting stuck. I was very disappointed and thought about how to do this. I continued to walk back in the big queue that had been formed by all vehicles. Then I saw a semi-trailer, i.e. a big lorry, I asked him, "can you help me and tow me", he replied to me in pure Australian, "no worries mate". He passed the entire queue of vehicles until he came in front of our car. I noticed that his exhaust pipe was just above the water level. I saw that someone had called for the tow truck, which stood before us further on dry land. He had an iron chain, which he attached under the engine of our car, while I was sitting behind the steering wheel, which turned on the ignition. He pulled out our entire vehicle as if it was a matchbox. Unfortunately, my engine did not give any symptoms to start, so he stopped when we had arrived on dry land and disconnected our car. I thanked him so much, and he said another "no worries mate".

Then the tow truck came to me and wanted to tow me to the nearest town, but I said I wanted to try to start the car during the towing. He plugged his rope under the engine again, and I turned on the ignition. He began to tow us, and it went metres by meter, and hundreds of metres with no results. The engine seemed completely dead, probably a lot of moisture around the breaker tips. Now we had safely driven a kilometre with an utterly dead engine when the engine suddenly started to "cough, cough, cough" and finally the engine was running. We stopped, but I did not dare to turn off the engine. He disconnected us, I paid him and thanked him.

I drove non-stop to Sydney, but we had to refuel on the road, and I did not dare to turn off the engine while refuelling. Finally, we had finished the 1020 km long way to Evans Street, Harbord. The next morning I couldn't start the car, it turned out that a lot of clay had been laying around the generator and had become hard like cement. We decided to change the car, and I saw a Chrysler Valiant Regal with a six-cylinder 4.9-litre engine. It cost about $6,000 and was white with a brown leather roof, with wide tyres and lowered to street level. Irmeli was in on the deal and also liked the car, so we bought it.

We received a letter from my mother in Sweden, where she told me that she had been anxious during our ventures in Queensland. My mother asked Jesus to save us, and she wondered what had happened. We wrote letters to her and told us what had happened to us.

New apartment in Allawah

The apartment started to be small when we had two children, so we started looking for a bigger apartment. It should have three bedrooms, living room, separate kitchen, laundry, hall, and storage room, as well as a garage. And in a price situation, we could afford it. It wasn't easy to find. Every weekend we went to various brokers who showed us new apartments. We went around in northern Sydney, and in southern Sydney, finally, Irmeli was tired of going up and down stairs looking for units. She asked me to do it. When she saw an apartment that had, e.g. a beautiful kitchen, so she stopped to admire it and did not think that it did not have, e.g. any storage or separate living room. Therefore, it took a lot of time for her, but I ruled it immediately out if the apartment did not qualify according to our wishes.

The following weekend I went alone to Kogarah, Allawah and Hurstville area, which was close to Sydney International Airport. I ran up and down the stairs at the new apartments, and checked out those that qualified. The result was that I found three apartments in Allawah that matched our requirements. I had decided on one of them but said nothing to Irmeli about what apartment it was. The following weekend I took with me Irmeli and began to show her the three flats. When we got into the last apartment, Irmeli stopped and looked at me and said, "This is the apartment!" I said, yes! It was a demonstration apartment, which had curtains, solid carpets, chandeliers. It cost $33,000, and that was precisely what we could afford. We signed the contract, and now we have to sell our apartment in Harbord. But the local broker could not sell it. Then we asked a Dee Why broker who was in a neighbouring suburb to sell the flat, and it was sold within a week, we earned $10,000 on it which was enough for the down payment on our new apartment in Allawah.

There is always board in those units, it must be appointed by the owners, and I was elected to be in this board. We would determine a maintenance levy to be paid, to cater for things such as painting, carpets, cleaning and a sinking fund for the exchange of worn equipment. I soon disagreed with especially a couple of brothers who lived in the apartment above us. To the extent that after a while we did not greet each other, but just stared straight ahead when we met and pretended not to see each other. It was mutual. I worked at Olivetti, and the office had moved to William Street. My sales district had been changed to the suburbs, and it was easier to go to my new customers. I was then promoted to the Special Account Representative and was awarded the largest customers in Sydney. Now I began to master the language better, and the language mistakes became fewer.

Joe's temptations

I had a colleague Joe, who started tempting me to sell his paintings. But I told Joe I am not interested. But Joe was stubborn, and he knew I had succeeded well with sales and was in the top 3 among Olivetti's salesmen. Joe invited me to lunch and discussed the sale of his paintings, and I rejected him again. Next time Joe took an oil painting with him to work and showed me. When I saw the art, I knew for sure that I was not interested. It was painted in strong colours. It was just landscape motifs of the Australian "bush". I said I could not sell these paintings, and no one will buy them. But Joe said it was effortless to sell, which I had difficulty in understanding. One day Joe came to me and said he had a fantastic deal to offer me, and we had another lunch again. Joe said if I could take a week's vacation from work, he would give me the whole car full of paintings, and it would be 110 paintings. The ones I was unable to sell, I could return, pay for what I sold. I said I'd think about it. I talked to Irmeli, and she thought I should try.

I gave a positive message to Joe. I took a week's vacation, and loaded the car with 110 paintings, besides the passenger seat, where Irmeli sat. We bought an order block and a calculator and decided to name IG Larsson after Irmeli. Then we headed north from Sydney right up to Lismore NSW, from there to Glen Innes and via the New England Highway back to Sydney. We visited furniture stores, chemists, and gift shops, e.g. We sold very well and only had one painting left for a week. Unfortunately, we stayed at the best hotels and ate the best food, so we spent all our profit.

But we had fun. Customers asked when we came back, and we said in three months. Then we had bound ourselves to sell regularly.

But I didn't want to stop working at Olivetti. So I asked Irmeli if she wanted to travel and sell the paintings. She said yes, and so it was, but there were a couple of issues. Irmeli did not have a driving license, and she had no car. She started training with me, and very soon, she was ready to drive. It went well for her, so she got the driving license. We bought a new Ford Escort passenger car.

Irmeli started selling paintings in the bush, we didn't sell any in Sydney, there was virtually no one selling paintings in the bush, so it went well. I taught Irmeli to sell paintings, but she didn't need a teacher, she was excellent. I gave her only one advice, "don't take a no for an answer!" Then she left. If the customer did not want to buy pictures anyway, she asked the customer "test the response with a few paintings", which the customer usually did. That's the way we started, we didn't like the paintings at all, but the customers loved them. It was logical for the customer to respond to the paintings in the store, and see if their customers bought the pictures. We also offered the customer to replace the arts if they were not sold, against other paintings, or products.

Irmeli had gained such momentum on the sale, so I discussed with Irmeli if I should stop working at Olivetti. She thought I should do it. Then I sold our Chrysler Valiant and got payment of pictures instead. I bought a Ford Transit that was large enough to accommodate more paintings. I worked on Olivetti for a while and now used the new Ford Transit in the job, while I filled it with pictures on weekends and went to nearby towns such as Windsor, Richmond and Penrith in the West, and Gosford, the Central Coast and Newcastle in the north. Sometimes I took the kids when I sold paintings so that they could ride horses or the like on Saturdays because there were activities for children along the roads.

The revenue began to rise and the time had come to resign at Olivetti and join the company, IG Larsson. We needed to expand our range and sought new suppliers. We found companies that framed prints, and also one that made the polyurethane wall plaques. They had to deliver their products to us, but only after I had bargained with them on their prices.
Sales continued and went very well, and it was time to repurchase more. Each time I bargained at their prices while buying larger quantities. Sometimes they were a little pressed, but because of that, I purchased more significant numbers, they accepted.

Most significant change in my life

My life transformation

Pastor Ruth Harvey

Trevor and Birgitta from Canberra continued to visit us. They came to Sydney at the end of March 1978, this time they called us and asked if we wanted to go to the Revival Life Centre in Penshurst (RLC), on a BBQ next Saturday. It is prevalent in Australia, and you very much want to attend a BBQ, it is very social, and usually pleasant and warm weather. Now we had booked something on this Saturday, so I answered Trevor that unfortunately, we were busy this Saturday. It was OK, Trevor said, and we ended the conversation.

The next morning, which was Sunday, Trevor called again, then I apologised so much for not being able to come. He responded quickly, and it does nothing because we meet today as well. Then I said we were going there, and it was before noon 11 in the morning.

We made arrangements with the children and went there. We saw that it was an old historic building that seemed interesting. Trevor invited us into the building and took us on tour, where we encountered a black-dressed older man who asked who this brother was. I was so amazed that I didn't know where to go and wished that there would be a trap door in the floor so that I could disappear quickly, I was not a brother But Trevor saved me and said I was a friend, thank you, Trevor. When we finished we stood in the doorway, Irmeli said, "I want to go in there", I checked what it was outside and I saw in my horror that there was a large tent behind the big bushy trees. I remembered the tent meetings in Sweden, where Pentecostal friends used to hold their meetings, my heart froze. But what could I say, I could not say that I did not dare go into the tent, so I swallowed my pride, and we went into the tent.

We sat at the back in the right corner for safety. Then I could make a quick escape later. Trevor also brought another Finnish family with him whom he introduced us, and it was Jouko and Kaarinna. In the middle of the long wall of the rectangular tent hung a long banner with the words "Jesus is coming soon". It caught me in the eye, and I thought what has Jesus to do with this. If one had written God instead of Jesus, it would have been more comfortable for the eyes. They started singing songs like: "Something good is going to happen, something good is in store". It was a short, powerful and very positive chorus they sang. Between the songs, some people came upon "platform" saying that they lost in drug and alcohol abuse. You could see on their faces that they had lived a tough life. But their eyes were full of love, joy and peace. We heard several testimonies. Then there was prayer, and there were people around us who prayed in a language we didn't know, it felt very uncomfortable, it made me want to run out. I had to hang on to stay. The prayer was mighty, and I had never before heard such a prayer. It touched powerfully, even though we didn't understand it. There were no empty words, but it seemed a definite spiritual meaning that we did not understand. The pastor began to preach, sometimes he said something I could not understand, it sounded like Arabic, I waited for the next time he would say some such words, and it came again, but I could not understand them. Then he suddenly looked in the left corner of the tent, he stretched out his arm and pointed in the right corner exactly where we were sitting, saying, "and you, you are just asking those questions, questions and questions. Stop asking questions and come to Jesus". I was shocked, after asking Trevor about six years, even most times we had sat up until the morning hours, but I had made no effort to decide to believe and accept Jesus. The sermon ended; the pastor was asking if anyone wanted to invite Jesus for the first time in their life. We sat still and didn't move. The meeting ended with singing and, when went out of the tent, there was someone in the tent opening shaking hands with us and asked what we were working with. I said we have our own company and sell prints. But honestly, I would have liked them to ask us spiritual questions. But they did not mention any other thing to us. We started to go to several other church meetings.

Jouko and Kaarinna invited us after the meeting. They were very friendly and had a young son. They lived in Revesby, which was not far from Allawah. I asked Jouko if he wanted to help us sell prints, and he said he could do that. I made some trips with him, so he learned how to sell the prints. He was a Christian and testified about Jesus to me on these journeys, after a while it became too much to hear, it felt so powerful that I could almost blow up if he didn't stop talking about Jesus. I changed the subject, and then the mood suddenly dropped, and I could breathe out. But right as it was, we were on the same issue again, and faith in Jesus came back, it became equally compelling in a while so I changed the subject again and could breathe out again. Jouko needed to buy a better car to sell prints, and he also purchased a Ford Transit.

RLC only had these tent meetings the first Sunday of the month, and in the meantime, we decided to go to Calvary Chapel, Greenacre, the pastor couple there were Don and Minta. The next Sunday we were there. We saw that they had a very youthful choir that sang. I thought that these beautiful young people did not have anything else they could do on a Sunday, but to be in a church and sing. The joy was glowing in their eyes, and I understood that they had something I didn't have. After the singing, came the sermon. This time, the preacher said something that touched us, and we wondered how he could know that about us. We hadn't talked to anyone, and no one knew us. Still, he said things that only we knew about ourselves. Our hearts were laid bare. It was very strange, and we hadn't been through this before. I began to feel a desire to be saved, as one says. When I was in the bathroom, I heard a voice within me saying: "When are you going to be saved, Curt" and I answered "Before I die", then the voice asked, "When do you die then, Curt"? I was equally surprised again, and I replied: "then I have to do it much earlier". Then I heard nothing more.

When I was on a business trip north, I remember thinking that if there were a church that had any meeting during the week, I wanted to go in and receive prayer to receive Jesus, because then no one would know about it.

I started reading the Bible in the morning in the motels, I set the alarm clock one hour earlier, and read one hour in the morning and one hour in the evening. For the most part, there was a Gideon Bible in the chest of drawers. But at some point the motel had no bible at all in the room and then I was disappointed. I started thinking about what I could hand over to Jesus, the company was OK, my family was OK, and then it was my beer drinking, and then I thought I could be a good Christian and drink beer, but my conscience was not convinced. In the end, I understood that I must give my whole life to Jesus, including my beer drinking.

Decision for Christ

We continued to go to different churches on Sundays until there was a tent meeting at the RLC again. This time, I had decided to go ahead and be saved; not even a locomotive could stop me. The pastor preached in the usual order, and then the invitation came to be saved, I raised my hand, so did my son Robert. But Irmeli asked him if he knew what he was doing, then he stayed in the pew. When I stood in front of the pastor, an older man got up from the first bench and laid his hands on my shoulders. The pastor put his hand on my head and began to pray, he asked me to say after him, when suddenly a thought came to me how can I believe that the Bible is true, I thought I did not have time to read the whole Bible and consider whether it was true or not, but said to God in my heart, "if this is your word, I accept it, but you have to show your word to me". During the prayer, I felt a force that I can resemble a six-volt battery flowing from the pastor's hand from head to my feet, but it was the same force that came out from the man behind me from his hands and down to my feet. After the prayer, the pastor said that it says in the Bible: "That if you shall confess with your mouth the Lord Jesus and shall believe in your heart that God has raised Him from the dead, you shall be saved". Then he asked me, "Do you believe in your heart that God has raised Jesus from the dead?" I replied "yes". Then he said "you have just confessed that Jesus is Lord, what must you be now," I replied, "saved"! He said yes, now you are a Christian.

I was filled with joy when the meeting was over, and I helped carry away all the chairs into the big building. There I met a lady in the doorway who gave me her hand and said "God bless you, you are a Christian now," I was thinking inside of me and said in my heart, yes I am because I have done it now!

Next week, we went to another church, and Irmeli gave

her life in Jesus' hands, and Camilla and Robert were also saved, later at a Billy Graham crusade.

My mother called and told me in the autumn, that Dad had worked with the garage wall, built of large stones when all of a sudden, the whole wall had fallen over him. He fainted and stayed on the ground alone. Mum was in town and did shopping. When she got home, she saw him lying there on the ground, rushed forward and laid her hands on dad and prayed. The ambulance came and took him to the hospital in Trollhättan. The next day, his head had swollen so he couldn't even open his eyes. They asked him how he felt, and he said OK. They asked him if he had any pain. He said no, no pain. It was extraordinary because he couldn't even open his eyes because of the significant swelling. I called him from Australia and talked to him. He seemed to feel good but just wanted to see how he looked, and dad had to wait until he could open his
 eyes, only to be able to look into a mirror.

Travel to Sweden in June 1978

We needed new products to sell. Because when we came back to a customer, and he did not need anything this time, we needed to sell something else in that place, we had the costs we had to cover. On the other hand, we did not want to sell the same products to another store because then there was a competition that was not popular in a small town. We came up with the idea of selling stainless steel kitchen products and chose a company in Sweden that sold kitchenware because of this, and they did not need any service. We

wanted an exclusive product to sell in Australia. We were looking for a name for our new company. We noticed that this factory in Sweden had a trademark registered that we liked. That name was Cultura. It was the right name for our company. We wanted to register Cultura as our new company name. They granted us their permission on the condition that we will not sell any bad quality stainless steel under that name. We promised and registered Cultura Pty Limited.
This time it was Irmeli's parents who had to look after our children while we were in Sweden.

We brought with us an assortment of our Australian prints, given possibly being able to export them to Sweden and Finland.

We first met my parents in Trollhättan. I was expecting an excellent opportunity to say that I had been saved. But when I finally told them about my experience with Jesus during a coffee time with my sister and my parents, my mother said, I already knew this when you came here. My mother also brought me to the prayer group in Halvordstorp in Trollhättan and introduced me. She said that this prayer group, with 30 people, had prayed for us many years that God would save us. Now they saw their prayers answered.

We met my other sister Miriam and Kjell in Sjuntorp. They asked a lot about Australia and were interested, and I also told how I experienced my meeting with Jesus, which they received!

Our trip to Sweden continued to Irmeli's sister and

husband in Eskilstuna, and then to Finland, where we visited various companies to sell our prints. Our exports did not go so well, only a few new customers in Sweden. We went back to Australia and our company. There our friend Jouko looked after our business.

Struck by lightning at church

I went to see Pastor Norm, and asked him, why is not somebody recording the services in the church. Pastor Norm said, "Do you want to do it, Curt"! I said, "if not anybody else is doing it, so will I do it". That's how I started with video in churches. On Sunday we had a torrential rain just before the service, I was sitting in my car on the church parking lot, and the rain was truly pouring down. It was a lot of thunders and lightening as well. The camera and recorder were in my lap. I thought that I have to put my coat over the equipment and run to the church door. It was about 30 metres. I opened the door to the car and ran towards the church door. I was struck by lightning about 7-10 metres away from the door, the flash covered me I glowed, I saw several other people also going into the church, and they saw me. I was like the time stood still for me, I felt nothing, then I remembered when I was about 10 years of age, when I was carrying milk in a 3 litre flask, when the lightning struck a tree about 7-10 metres away from me, and it split the tree, and I shook from power of the flash. I came to the door and was asked immediately to witness what had happened to me. I stepped up on the platform and testified, but I felt nothing. I believe now that God can protect from anything. Glory to God, who saved me.

An agent enters the store.

A man came into our shop and wanted to sell our products. He looked around first and then he said he wanted to try to work for us as an agent, i.e. he would buy an assortment and then sell it and come back and replenish. When he had selected what he wanted, we wrote out the invoice and asked him to pay by cheque, but he did not want it, but said he would deposit money in our bank account first and wait until we confirm that we have received the payment Then he would come and fetch it at the warehouse. It sounded perfect, so we did. When he had sold out after a while, he came back, and the procedure was the same, no problems at all. But then he had a small problem and could not pay everything in advance. We had now gained some confidence in him and gave him credit. He paid off this delivery, and we sold further to him, but it was more and more difficult for him to pay, and finally he owed a lot of money. We didn't hear from him either. We checked him out and found that he had made several such transactions with other companies. It was harder and harder to cope because of this loss. And I blame myself for this. We prayed to God for help. We adhered to our giving in the congregation, and I choose to be faithful to God despite this great disappointment.

Prophecy in church

It was a very unusual prophecy. Someone gave a prophecy in our church, about how God would supply our needs in a very particular way. Some things we get at a very reduced price, and other stuff for nothing. It was just a prophecy that was for anybody who received it. And I received it. One man came in and asked if we were interested in a bankruptcy stock of silk flowers. He wanted to sell for $7,000. It was a lot of money for us right now, and we asked to think about it and return in a few days. The tall Peter came in, and we asked him about this offer. We felt this was from God, so we decided to buy this stock. We charged 100% and would sell them for double the price. There were many kinds of flowers, from orchids, roses, green plants, bouquets etc. We contacted some flower shops, and they brought their vans and looked. They were very impressed and bought a lot. They carried out as much as they could and filled their van. This went very well. But they said our prices were meagre. Then we added 600%, and the prices were still low, it was a great blessing from God. We recovered much faster now, and we bought several times from the bankruptcy administrator. And the flowers sold like butter in the sunshine. Proverbs 13:22 "A good man leaveth an inheritance to his children's children: and the wealth of the sinner is laid up for the just."

Repair of gearbox free of charge

We needed to service the automatic gearbox on our Ford Transit, just before Easter. I had booked it in in a large Australia wide company at their workshop in Bankstown. When I came here on Thursday before Easter to pick it up, I went to the man who was standing in the middle of the workshop and asked him how much it cost, and then he said nothing. I did not believe him, so I went to the office to pay the bill, I asked the girl how much it was, she did not know, but walked out from the back of the office and I could follow her with my eyes through the glass windows, as she walked up to the same man. He just shook his head, then she came back and said, there was no charge. I thanked her and took the van.

Jouko took this van on a trip to Queensland, after Easter. But when he was in Mt. Isa, he rang me and said that the gearbox had broken down and it cost $1500 to fix it. I rang up the company in Bankstown and asked them what do I do. They said that I should pay the bill and send it to them. The next weekend Jouko rang me again from Townsville and told me that the gearbox had broken down again. I rang the company in Bankstown again and asked what shall I do. They said that they would fly up to a technician and another gearbox, and work on the van the whole weekend. Which they did, and the van was ready to drive on Monday morning. All this cost me nothing, according to the word of the Lord. Now Jouko and I went on a trip to Bourke, Charleville, Winton, Mt. Isa, Townsville and then non-stop to Sydney. Just before Bourke, I ran over a sheep, and it just became a soft canister under the van, no damage to the vehicle, but the sheep were hurt. The roads are usually very straight out in the bush, so we saw something that looked very strange, far away in the distance approaching. We couldn't figure out what it was even though we were approaching. It was a coyote, one that they had on the prairies in the United States with a round roof covered in cloth. It was a big David's star at the front of the carriageway opening. He had two camels pulling it, and a young camel walking alongside. Inside the cart had a kitchen and sleeping area. The camels strolled on the road and did not turn aside; he could then do other chores during the journey and did not have to check the path. One can say that the camels were on "Cruise Control". When the camels came to a "grid" it was like a railway track that went across the road to stop livestock, then the camels stopped, he had a large plywood disc which he put on the rails, then the camels went over. We asked to have a ride with him for a short distance, and after the trip, we walked back to our van.

I once crashed with a kangaroo near Charleville. The strange thing was that it would jump up from the road in front of me, and then jumped back into the bush, and then once again, the kangaroo rushed straight into the van. It struck my headlights, and it was pitch dark, and it became challenging to drive back to the city to get new lights the next day.

When we were in Winton, we found out that the road was off towards Cloncurry, a distance of 350 km, when we consulted the police about which way we could go. They said we could go through Hughenden, a detour of 270 km. They said we had to watch out for potholes on the road, and they could cause the axles to break if one was travelling too fast. We drove, and in the beginning, it went well, the road was, and there was dirt road all the way. The railway was parallel to the road. Soon there was water and holes on the road we kept a speed of about 60 km/h, and then we suddenly saw all the way covered with water. We drove off the road where there was no water but got stuck in the mud. We started digging out with just the hands, and then we went to the railway which was 20 metres away from us and picked up gravel, we only had a newspaper to carry the gravel. While we were doing this, we saw a freight train coming very slowly, and it seemed it would stop because it slowed down. Right that we would get help. But you should not shout hello until you were over the brook when the train was almost there, it increased in speed, and the drivers just waved to us. When we had collected enough gravel, we attempted with the van, and we came loose. We then drove up to the road and had a lake in front of us, we went out to investigate, it was not deep, but it was muddy. We decided to find a lot of rocks and make two wheel tracks with the stones so that I could drive on them. Then I carried out the two short planks I had with me, to use in such situations. When I considered that we had worked enough, I told Jouko to drive. He said "never" Curt, you drive. He didn't want to risk getting stuck with the van. OK, I reversed to get some more speed to take off. I had relatively high speed under the circumstances drove up on the stone tracks that we had built up, but then the van almost stopped and partly slipped off the rails, I managed to steer the van back to dry ground. Pooh !!

Sauna competition

Jouko was a Finn and liked to go to the sauna, and he used to stay with Finns, who was always so hospitable. He called his friend in Mt. Isa and asked in Finnish if they can heat the sauna, so we can have a sauna when we got there. They would. When we arrived, they welcomed us and invited us to change and stay with them. The sauna was only temporary made in the garden. The walls were of canvas, and there were two rooms, one with wash basin and shower, and then the sauna itself. I was a long time inside the sauna, and they spoke Finnish so that I couldn't keep up. One after the other, they disappeared, at last, it was just me left, and then I went out. The Finn laughed when I came out because they said they had burned everything so that they couldn't stay longer. The Finn hoped that it would be so hot that I would leave the sauna.

Miriam and Kjell were emigrating.

My sister Miriam and her husband Kjell had decided to also emigrate to Australia, they came to Sydney on February 1, 1979, with their two children. They bought a house eventually in Green Valley outside Liverpool in Sydney. And Kjell got a good job. It was a Billy Graham Crusade at Randwick's Race Course in Sydney from April 29 to May 20, 1979. We went there with Miriam and Kjell and the kids. There were a lot of people tens of thousands. Think it was about 90,000 that came every time. Many lives were changed when people received Jesus as their Saviour. Many were born again when they accepted Jesus as their Saviour. About 57,000 received Jesus, which was 5% of Sydney's population at the time. Crime and birth rates were sharply reduced according to statistics several years later. The Crusades he made in Australia for many years have ultimately affected 2% of Australia's population who have been reborn through faith in Jesus.

Dealing with Dennis

We continued to sell prints and stainless steel kitchen products. But to sell the stainless steel, we needed an attractive display stand for the stores. We wanted the entire assortment shown in the stores. We asked one of our suppliers who made products with a velvet-like surface, and this company was called Artecon. We chose a blue colour and ordered a stand with three shelves and a sign at the top. Now we were able to sell a whole package to the stores, and then sales went even better. I received a quote from Dennis, who was the manager of Artecon, and I accepted directly without bargaining.

I bought more and more products from Artecon, and I thought his prices were reasonable, so I always accepted it directly without haggling. The next time I came to Dennis to buy new products, he gave me a quote again, which I took immediately. Then Dennis asked, "What happened to you". I thought that it is probably no idea that I tell you about Jesus, for he would not believe that, so I did not give him an answer. I used to visit him about every two weeks. On the next visit the same thing happened, when he gave me a quote, I accepted the price, with a smile. Then Dennis stamped with his foot on the floor and asked me "what has happened to you, Curt". I thought now you are requesting and I will give you a correct answer. I said: "Jesus has saved me". Then Dennis said: "I believe you". I asked Dennis, "Why"? Dennis answered me, "because you no longer bargain with me, only accept my quote with a smile". I asked Dennis to come with me to my church, which he did, and he got saved. Then the same thing happened with his foreman, who saw the change in Dennis life, and asked him what happened to him. The result was that they were both baptised in water in my church.

Big order of dishes

We decided to participate in another exhibition, we used to participate in shows about every two years, and they had always given us new customers. But this time I asked Irmeli, should we pray to God that he gives us three times the record, we prayed a simple prayer that God would provide us with three times the record, and so AMEN. At this exhibition, we sold stainless steel and prints to companies, not to private people. Irmeli was very good as a sales associate and had received a large retail chain store as a customer, and they wanted to order many packages of stainless to their stores. Now I made a mistake because I did not want to deliver free of charge to all their stores, and we lost this order because of me, and I regret it. Sometimes you can be hung up on details, and not see the big picture.

A man came in on Sunday, and was interested in our oval serving dishes, and he requested a quote for several thousand serving dishes.

I started to figure out the price of all the dishes, and it would be a big order. Then I got the idea that if I would only add 10%, it would still be an excellent profit. Then I felt an inner voice telling me, "Curt, I want you to make a reasonable profit". OK, I thought, I add on 50% then and posted the quote. When we counted the turn over we had received almost three times the record, with about 20% was missing from 300%. Then I reminded God that when we prayed, we believed, and so we got what we asked for, even though it was 20% missing. The time went on by, and week by week I got these thoughts, "you should not believe that you get these three times the record", then I replied: "When I prayed, so I believed; therefore I have already received the answer". These thoughts regularly came for about nine months, when I suddenly got a phone call when I was sitting at my desk in the office. He who called asked, "Are you sitting down, Curt"? I said, "yes, I am". He told me he wanted to place an order with me on these thousands of serving dishes. And that this order was the first in a three years contract. And it would turn out in three years that the contract was renewed for another term of three more years.

This first order, along with the sales from the exhibition became three times three of what we had asked God. God had multiplied my prayer by three times. Must say God is good, always. He explained to me that the Australian government is not looking at the price so much, but is looking more at the Australian content of the total amount. With my 50% profit margin, plus my customer's margin, who would polish the dishes in Australia, were included then, the Swedish part became much less than 50%. If I would have added 10%, then I would have lost the order.

The next day I was ready to fax the order to Sweden, but then my customer called again, and said that he had read through the contract and found that he cannot buy through a local importer, but must buy directly from Sweden, he offered me a small commission instead. I did not feel good, and I remember a saying that says, "Proverbs 15:22 Without counsel purposes are disappointed: but in the multitude of counsellors they are established."

Then I first called up my accountant and told the story. He said, "Curt just sit there and wait".
After that, I called Pastor Norm, told him everything, but not what advice I already received, then he told me, "Curt just sit there and wait".

Then I called up a state government purchasing officer in another department and said the same story, the officer said, "Curt just sit there and wait".
After a few days, my customer called again, first then he apologised, and said he had misunderstood the

contract, and he could undoubtedly buy through me.
I placed the order with Silver and Steel. Then they told me that my customer had called them and said that he wanted to order these serving dishes from them. Then they answered him that they have an agent in Sydney called Curt Larsson, and if he contacted me, then I would order them for him. So he got a NO from our Swedish manufacturer, and had no other option but to humbly call me and place the order. Another thing he was aware of was that these dishes would have an open edge, that is, not an edge that was folded in, because then dirt and bacteria could be collected there. All his dishes had a folded edge, and only my dishes had an open corner. Therefore, he could not sell his dishes. It was an old and established company. The delivery came, and I had requested a letter of credit, as a guarantee for payment. The orders from my customer rolled on, and they were quite large, but now his finances were such that he did not have the financial strength any more to guarantee payment by letter of credit, so he asked if he could soon sign over the contract to me, so then I had "Logistic Command" as my customer, that is, Australia's defence. And they paid with Master Card, "cash". Now it was he who "got the commission" and I billed the security. So it can be if you are not satisfied with what
 you get but want more.

Mark is starting to work.

Martin came to me after the church morning service and asked me if I had a job for his son Mark. I used to go to Martins place on Saturday morning prayer, and he always prayed for his two sons. I told him to ask Mark to come down to the office at 10 am on Monday. When he arrived, I interviewed him, and he seemed to be eager to try out. I said we were going to Rockhampton in Queensland and then to Keppel Island and bathing, but on Sunday we are going to church. He accepted this. And next week we went away to Queensland. During the trip, I played many Christian music cassettes. I had a favourite called Buzz Goertzen from Idaho. He was a former policeman who was Christian yodelling singer. What I didn't know then was that Mark hated yodelling. We had a perfect time in the van and enjoyed each other.

We reached Rockhampton on Friday night and checked in at a campsite. We went out to Keppel Island the next day, and went by boat with a sport called "Boom netting". Two bars were hanging straight out on one side with a large net between them that also reached down over the water surface. The trick was that when someone went out on the boom and descended into the net, they would also stick to the net. Then suddenly the captain gasped, and if you did not have a waistband around the waist, you lost the swimwear and became naked. Then the audience applauded. But it went well for Mark. After lunch and snorkelling, we were ready and went back.

We were in church on Sunday at 11, and it was a beautiful song of praise, with much harmony. Mark stood next to me, and suddenly, Mark began to speak in tongues in the song of praise. The pastor was bold and said that now we would follow him around the church while walking first and holding the Australian flag. It was lively.

From there, we returned via Brisbane and this time the New England Highway via Tamworth to Sydney. We were in Tamworth on Saturday morning, and I needed to sell on Saturday to cover the costs. I visited a gift shop full of people. Then God told me to pray for the owner, who was entirely white in the face. I said no, I would not do that. Again the call came for her. I told OK, you say it, but not me. I asked if I could pray for her, and she answered yes. It a lot of people in there, and I prayed for her. Immediately she felt better and rushed to the mirror on the wall and said that she had been healed. After that, we went straight to Sydney. Mark started working with us, and he brought his mother out a few times. His experience with Jesus in Rockhampton had touched him so much that he wanted to study to become a pastor. Then Mark left us and started Bible school.

Trip to Sweden via Hawaii

We now wanted to expand our sales to Sweden and Scandinavia and decided to go back to Sweden. This time we went across the US and Hawaii, it was the first time we went that route. We stayed in Hawaii for a week and looked at the sights, especially the "Polynesian Cultural Centre", Waikiki Beach and Pearl Harbour and the USS Arizona Memorial. The temperature is around + 30C throughout the year, wonderful climate.

We had a "stopover" in Los Angeles, with visits to

Disneyland and the great churches, such as "The Glass Cathedral" and "Church on the Way", which was Pat Boone's Church. We went up to San Francisco and greeted one of my salesman Philip and his wife. After this we stopped in Memphis, Irmeli wanted to look at Elvis's house and aircraft. Back to Sweden, where my cousin Lasse and Ulla were waiting at Landvetter to drive us to Trollhättan where the family was waiting with a warm welcome and even made a sign above the front door. It was a great welcome and very friendly. Thanks to Lisbeth and Svein and everyone else who was there and made our day memorable. We had bought a used Volvo from a car company in Vänersborg, which we used for travelling. But we wanted to visit Lasse and Ulla before. Late in the afternoon after our visit, we drove back to Trollhättan, but I noticed that on the narrow paved road a car came from the front on the "wrong side". I flashed my headlights and kept to the left as much as I could, but the other driver seemed to be stubborn and didn't want to change to the other side of the road. Even at the last second, he was still as stubborn and did not yield. I was then forced to drive in the left ditch. I went to the car, and there sat a young man in his mid 20s and just trembled non-stop. Then it dawned on me that it was I who had driven on the wrong side (left). I excused myself so much and explained that I came from Australia where you drove on the left side, and then we drove over to the right and continued to Trollhättan. We visited Silver & Steel in Vingåker, which delivered steel to us and discussed new products. Then it was time to go back.

We had now agents who sold for us in Melbourne and Brisbane. Jouko worked from Sydney.

Journey with Jouko to WA

We decided that Jouko and I would go to Western Australia and sell. It's a long trip just to Perth. It's about 3950 km. We packed our Ford Transit full, so you could barely fit a matchbox anywhere. And then we hired a trailer, which we loaded with about 1 ton of prints. We started the journey from Sydney and made our way across Broken Hill, but first, we would cross the Blue Mountains right on the outskirts of Sydney. Blue Mountain is at an altitude of about 1100 metres. The road was getting steep and progessively steeper, and in the beginning it went well, but now the sounds coming from the engine were a growing concern, it slowed down so much that Jouko had to switch to first gear before we got to the crest, but now it sounded seriously in the engine, it almost stopped, you could hear how the pistons moved slowly in the engine, and we could clearly count the strokes. We were at full throttle, it was a significant drop of hundreds of metres behind us and the brakes would not be enough to stop the van, and if we did we would risk losing everything. The engine eventually almost finished, but when the road smoothed out slightly, and the slope decreased, we approached the crest very slowly. We counted the seconds. The engine was now gradually increasing, more and more. We started to be happy, and in the end, we were on the crest, and the stress was over. The journey continued over desert districts. We had two spare jerry cans with us, every 20 litres. We could only drive 200 km on a tank, and there was usually a petrol station every 200 km. We started our sale along the trip to Perth when we arrived at Ceduna in South Australia, so there was a long straight stretch of 1200 km, no villages, only petrol stations every 200 km, where we ran over a wombat which is as big as a pig, only with fur. There were no injuries, but it smelled roasted pork a reasonable time after that.

We finally arrived in Norseman and got to sell a little there. Now we headed north towards Kalgoorlie about 190 km, which is a mining town, where you dig for gold. The van did not go so well, we finally came to a halt with the truck, beside the road. We couldn't start the trailer. It was in a desert area, and no people or houses were there, not much traffic. In the end, a coach arrived, which stopped for us. Thank God for that. He had no towing line, but we had a short rope of about two metres behind the bus. We told him to slow down very slowly because we had no brakes, only used the gears as brakes. The engine must be running for the brakes to work. Otherwise, you have to step very hard on the pedals. He promised to slow down slowly when we arrived at a workshop. Jouko didn't want to drive the van, so I had to do it.

The coach started driving pretty fast, and it was tough to maintain safety by steering just two metres away from the rear of the coach, we began to get a little scared and said that soon we would meet Jesus. If the coach were to break in, we would be squeezed in because our trailer was loaded with a ton and the Ford Transit had a tiny bonnet, half of the engine were in the van. I started to reel out to the right and stretching out my arm and waving, so he would slow down, the speed was about 100 km/h, just too fast not to collide with him with a margin of two metres. I waved many times without results. The driver did not notice anything, this was difficult. There were many cars driving towards where we were going. Then the driver slowed down a little, and then a little more, and a little more, after several kilometres, we were stationary outside a workshop. We left the van, and the driver excused himself and said he had forgotten us in the back. We said it was OK. When the van was repaired, sales continued, through the towns out in the village until we arrived in Perth. There we went to Miss Maud's restaurant. It is a Swedish lady who started selling cinnamon buns and other Swedish pastries, which became so popular that she expanded into a restaurant with Danish and Swedish chefs. We ate a delicious Swedish smorgasbord and treated us to this luxury after the long desert journey.

We went up to the coast in the north, to Port Headland, it was 610 km to the next town, and then another 1870 km to Darwin. We decided it was not financially viable.

We headed south from Port Headland towards Marble Bar, which is only 200 km away, with a population of 240 people. It's Australia's second hottest spot, and we drove through in the spring. Not much to do there, we continued south 300 km towards Newman, we arrived late in the afternoon, and it was time to book into a room for the night. We first went to a campsite that hired out caravans overnight. It is widespread and cheaper than hotel rooms. But they were fully booked and said that if there is no room anywhere else, we could check with them again. After asking around the city, there was no room for us. We went back to the campsite and asked again, he said it is still full, but then he suddenly said wait a bit, and he disappeared in his office. He came back and said to us, "Follow me". Then I said to Jouko in Swedish. We would certainly get the biggest and best caravan. He stayed outside a large caravan, which had air conditioning in the ceiling. We asked how much we would pay. Then he said it cost one dollar, which covers the electricity. Thank you, dear God!

Newman was another mining town. We continued south when we had finished our work there. Soon we were back in Perth, and from there we went south to Bunbury and from there to Albany on the south coast, and then to Norseman in the west, it was this time all wild spring flowers were blooming, it was one of the most amazing experiences, because the flowers could be tiny and beautiful or up to the size of shrubs and trees in all the colours of heaven. Which are rarely seen anywhere else in the world? Sometimes we have to stop and look at the unusual flowers. I strongly recommend the journey between Perth and Norseman via the south coast in September - October. When we came to Norseman again, we practically had nothing left of our stock and resorted to taking a lot of orders. Now, only the long journey of 3950 km remained to Sydney, so we were about to take turns in sleeping, we changed over at the next petrol station. It took about three days before we were back in Sydney. But just before we arrived the van stopped on the Hume Highway in an inner Sydney city suburb, we could no longer start the car. The engine had burnt out; this long journey of about 11000 km was too much for our van. We had to change out the the engine.

The tall Peter

We hired more sales staff and office staff, but I opted to hire everyone through the church because it is better to give a glass of cold water in the name of a disciple, and to the least of mine, said Jesus, we could pray together, and we all had the same joy. Peter who was a former millionaire, from England, but had lost almost all his money and needed a job. He was 2.07 metres tall and needed no ladder when we were to hang up prints in the stores. He liked to talk about Jesus with the customers, and they listened to him. I remember when we went to Canberra where we had booked into a motel. We had two separate beds in the room, and when I saw his legs stick out under the sheets over the end of the bed, I couldn't hold myself for laughing. He understood what I was laughing at, and said this is a common experience for him, as most beds are only 2 metres, and he wants to have his head slightly on the edge of the bed as well.

Healed from nose bleeding

It was on another trip to Canberra when I was having a big problem with nose bleeding. Every morning when I woke up and would get out of bed, the nose started to bleed. When I was a boy, I often had nose bleeding problems, especially when I was playing with other children, and then had to lie down straight until the nose bleeding had stopped. The doctors had administered a burning method 10 times in order to prevent the nose from bleeding, and the last time the doctor burned me, he said that if it bleeds again, they can't do anything more for me. It was these words that rang in my ears now in Canberra. I started selling as usual in the morning and came to a Christian book store. We also sold Christian prints with Jesus and last supper, among other things. The owner asked me if I should go to the Full Gospel Business Mens Fellowship International dinner in the evening. They regurlarly organise dinners and also invite someone to speak or testify, but rarely any priest. It was an American military who would speak in the evening.

I went there and listened, after his speech he invited those who wanted prayers. Then I put myself in the queue. Various ailments healed several. When it was my turn, he asked what it was that I wanted him to pray about. I said I have nosebleeds. Then he said that he would not pray for me. I felt very disappointed and thought it took forever to hear what he said next.

"<u>Read Ezekiel 16: 6</u>, **And when I passed by thee, and saw thee polluted in thine own blood, I said unto thee when thou wast in thy blood, Live; yea, I said unto thee when thou wast in thy blood, Live.**"

I thought then if this is all I would get, then I should read this verse and before they close the lid of the coffin, I would shout this verse. Back at the motel, I opened the Bible and read this verse until I knew it off by heart.

The next morning when I woke up, guess what happened, no you guessed wrong. I bled as much, but now I had the word in my heart. I went into the bathroom and looked at me in the mirror and quoted this Bible verse while I pointed to myself in the mirror and added: "It is written... "And when I passed by thee and saw thee polluted in thine own blood, I said unto thee when thou wast in thy blood, Live; yea, I said unto thee when thou wast in thy blood, Live."
After maybe 10 minutes, the nosebleed stopped, and I never had that problem anymore.

I have passed this on twice to others who have suffered from nosebleeds. To a younger boy in church, who was part of a Sunday school presentation to the congregation, he began to bleed and cry on the platform. It touched my heart, and I talked to him afterwards and gave him instructions on what to do. Learn the Bible word by heart and say, "It's written ...... Ezekiel 16:6". After that, I did not see him in the church for several years yet he came back when he was older. I had a hard time recognising him, so I asked his father if it was him, and he said yes. So I asked if he remembered me, and he did. I wondered about what happened to his nosebleed problem. He said he never had more issues with nosebleed because God is watching over His word to perform it! Be encouraged!

Healed from gallstone attacks

I liked to eat the Swedish crisp bread "Wasa" with

cheese slices on top, we bought Wasa bread from the importer and sold some to Swedes. It had evolved into a horrible experience. I ate many crisp bread sandwiches with cheese. I got a couple of atrocious gallstone attacks, and I had a lot of pain. I went to the hospital, they treated me in the emergency room, and they wanted to operate me. The so-called keyhole operation, but I said no to it. Asked what other options did I have. They said I had to eat a tablet every day for the rest of my life.
I said, "I don't want to do that".
They said there is no other option.
I said, "Yes, there is, Jesus would heal me".
They laughed at me in disbelief. I also got two injections with 20 mg of morphine for the excruciating pain, which did not help. The doctor tried to persuade me to operate, but I refused.
When I got home, I googled about gallstone attacks and alternative treatment. I did not like the word "alternative", I like the word original, but since all the answers I received contained apple juice and olive oil, I then stopped eating food, and bought green apples and made juice in our juice extractor, not in a mixer, it must be a juice extractor, if you eat the whole apple you can die, so it is essential to make juice, and drink the strained juice without the "pulp". And I took a tablespoon of olive oil for bedtime, every night. After three days, I did not feel any gallstones symptoms, but continued for 14 days, on the last day, I took a glass of olive oil, which was almost impossible to get down. I spewed it up before I had swallowed it all. Then I mixed it with grape juice, and then I could drink a whole glass of olive oil. Besides, I took a glass of

Epson salt dissolved in warm water. The next day I almost stayed in the toilet, all the gallstones came out and did not get stuck because of olive oil I had taken all the time. It was about 25 years ago, and I have never had any gallstone attacks. I live a healthy life now with all my organs. Thank you, Jesus. Do not copy what I did; seek doctors medical advice! Always check with your doctor.

Riding on the back of a truck

Irmeli and I went up to the coast to Townsville then via Mt. Isa and down to Winton via Charleville to Sydney. When we were in Winton, they told us that it had started raining a few days ago farther east, and the water would drain into the rivers any time, and the road to Charleville would be cut off, because of this flooding. Our van would not be able to withstand the deep water. Then someone said that we could drive up our van on the back of a truck. But how would we get our van up there? We were told to go to where they load livestock because you can drive up on the ramp, and then on the back of the truck. It went well, and it was 700 km to Charlieville. We were three with the driver in the truck, everything went well, but when we came to Charlieville, the water was already high. The driver said it would probably be fine. There was a hairline margin. We drove through the river, which is not usually a river at all.

School holidays in Cairns

When it was school break for the kids, we went on a

long trip up to Cairns in northern Queensland, where it was always summer, and we could go out to the Great Barrier Reef and snorkel and swim. We had souvenirs that we were selling on the islands. It was a good idea to make some money by selling souvenirs so that we could visit some tourist attractions. The kids also wanted to sell prints, so I let them into a store, and they did not want me to follow them in, but they wanted to sell prints on their own accord. They got an order placed for pictures, and they were pleased and encouraged. Camilla needed to start school, so we flew her back to Sydney to get to school in time, while Robert had finished school and had begun training as a pastry chef, and therefore did not need to start until later, he thus remained with us back to Sydney.

Olivetti agency

I had started selling Olivetti computers, had an agency by Olivetti, and had to buy four computers at once, which I would sell. My salesman bought one, and he had a friend who purchased another from me. Then one of my suppliers purchased a computer, but he wanted such a great discount that I finally said then you would have to give me a large framed painting that I can hang on my wall. After a while, it was time to choose a picture frame. His brother was there alone on the day when I wanted to choose a picture frame. Then I decided on a small cheap frame because I didn't want it to be too expensive for him. But he said, it won't be nice, you should have this picture frame, and he showed one of the most expensive frames. I paused a little, but when he insisted, I accepted that frame. I received the framed painting after about a week, and I received an invoice for the picture frame. Then I said that we had agreed that I would get the oil on canvas with a picture frame, the other brother then said it was ok. I was very pleased.

Our greatest difficulties

1984 a year of sorrow

Irmeli had recurring dreams. She saw in her dream four coffins were stacked upon each other. We prayed about this but did not understand who was in the coffins. The other recurring dream was a star appearing from a distance, drawing very near, and finally disappearing, one by one. There were four stars in total.

Irmeli's brother Tommi died suddenly in May. Tommi was just under 50 years of age. We couldn't go to Sweden for the funeral, Tauno and Outi grieved a lot for their eldest son. One expects the children to live longer than their parents. Tommi had four children.

Tauno also had a long term problem with his lungs, and at that time he was in the Royal North Shore Hospital in Sydney. Outi visited him very often and also Irmeli. I had witnessed to him about my experience with Jesus, and he said "He had drunk the blood (last supper) and he was saved", due to that. I had such a burden for him to receive Jesus and did not know what to do. Then I prayed for him to see Jesus' glory before he died, that was the only thing I could do. When Irmeli was there he became so sick that he died, then Irmeli told the doctors to give him an adrenaline injection in his heart.

The doctor said, "Who is the doctor here"?
Irmeli noted, "It's about my father, do as I tell you".

Then the doctor gave him an adrenaline injection in his the heart, and Tauno woke up, but he was angry. He said, "Why did you wake me up. I have seen God now". Tauno lived a few more weeks, and Irmeli prayed to God for him, and he received Jesus!

On July 12, 1984, Tauno departed from us, and the grief became even more significant because we also grieved for Tommi. Robert was very sad that his grandfather had passed away. Outi moved to us and got an apartment in Carlton. She enjoyed that place thoroughly. It was only two kilometres to her. She wanted to pray with us every day at the dinner table. Robert continued to study and practice baking pastry. He made adorable cakes at home. Robert could sit for hours decorating a cake, with joy and great patience. He travelled to school from Allawah to Epping and had to change trains in the city.

Robert dies in a train accident

I got a vision one evening, where I saw a light shine that I perceived as Jesus.
He asked me, "Can I have your son?"
I answered, "No".
Then I saw the darkness that wanted to take Robert.
I said, "You can't have him".
Again I saw the light asking, "Can I have your son?"
I said, "No"?
Again I saw the darkness that wanted to take Robert, I said, "You can't have him"?
A third time I saw the light that asked:
"Can I have your son?"
Then I answered, "If there is no other way, then you have my son".
The days went by, and I finally forgot about this vision.

On the ninth of October, I was about to go on a business trip out in the bush, the last customer before I left Sydney, just before I was going drive across to the Blue Mountains. I was visiting a customer who had bought a computer with programs, and I was giving them software and hardware training. Their phone rang in the office. They said it was for me. It was Irmeli who was crying, and she could hardly get the words out. Irmeli told me that Robert was dead! I said it couldn't be right. Irmeli said I have to come home quickly. I told the customer that I had to cancel and go back. I cried all the way home in the van. When I got home, Irmeli sat on the couch and cried. Irmeli told me that, Robert came to the bedroom in the morning, he told her about his plans, and what he was going to do for Christmas.

Then he went up to the train station in Allawah and took the train as usual. When the train had driven two stations, the doors flung open, and Robert flew out and hit his head on the stanchion and died instantly. The police came knocking on the door, and Irmeli opened, they said our son Robert was dead. She got such a shock that she almost fainted. They asked her to go to the hospital and identify him. When she got there she saw him through the glass, then Irmeli asked them to open so that she could enter. They said that they usually never do, but when she insisted they opened the door. Robert had great peace, Irmeli knew Robert was not there. She prayed a prayer and went home. Irmeli also later explained that God's peace filled that room.

This accident caused an outcry in Sydney and throughout Australia, because this was the 17th accident of the same kind in Sydney, the year 1984, namely that the doors of the trains flung open during the journey and passengers fell out of the trains. They had long complained about the maintenance, and that they had to shape up. His photo appeared on the first page of The Sun and Daily Mirror. Channel Nine News broadcast Roberts death accident across Australia. Our congregation got a shock and prayed intensely for us. Then we felt surrounded by angels. The pastors came home to us. We almost couldn't rise from the couch. The burden was heavy to carry. At that moment I told Irmeli, we can't change what has happened, why should we not thank God that Robert is with God. And we began to thank God, then lifted the heavy cutting grief for a while. But then it came back with full force again, we praised God again, and the dense cloud lifted us. In between, the doorbell rang, and parishioners came, one after another. They always had a comforting word to us, and we felt uplifted. It was like a fresh breeze every time the doorbell rang. But we stayed on the couch and struggled with this great grief, first Tommi, then Tauno then our son. We refused to give up and continued to thank God for knowing the best. After a few weeks, we came up "to the surface", so we could breathe emotionally.

Then I got a revelation that I would not see my dad any more. I called Sweden and talked to my dad, and told him that God had shown me that we would not meet any more, and encouraged him to spend time with Jesus and praise his name. Dad was active in his faith and often went to his brothers on his moped and witness about Jesus. On 1st November 1984, we were told that my father had gone home to Jesus. He had taken it hard when his only grandson had died. He was on his way, through the hospital park, on his bicycle to Lisbeth to pick up a tool for sharpening millstones, when he suddenly fell off onto the bicycle track and had a heart attack and died immediately, a dog found him and kept barking until the dog owner arrived, who then immediately called the police.

Travel to the funerals

One of our church members had a travel agency, and he offered us a trip to Sweden at a very generous price. It was October and time to go to my dad's funeral 1st November. So Irmeli, Camilla, Outi and I prepared for this trip to Sweden via Rome. I remember when we arrived in Rome and stayed at a hotel for a couple of days. We were too tired that we slept for 12 hours. We had 14 suitcases, and only Camilla and I could carry them, we had to shuttle back and forth while Irmeli waited in one end and Outi in the other end. We managed very well, Camilla was very good at helping. We visited the Colosseum in Rome, but I felt the spirit of murder there.
We continued to my dad's funeral and then celebrating Christmas in Sweden with my mother and Outi with her daughter and family up in Eskilstuna. I would catch up with Irmeli and Outi in Eskilstuna after Christmas.

Elida

Mum told me that Elida was in Trollhättan, we didn't know about this boat, but went there Elida offered coffee and buns to all visitors. Tarren who was the skipper, greeted us and asked about us who we were etc. we told our sad story, then he invited us to come on board Elida for a few days, from the port of Gothenburg after the funeral. We went down to

Gothenburg and went on board Elida. It was an experience, an utterly Christian boat that only had a motto, to sing and tell about what Jesus did, and what Jesus does today. Tarren was a former car dealer who had been saved from alcoholism one Christmas Eve many years ago. He used the boat as a platform to reach people, out in the Swedish waters, and which nowadays also goes as far as the Canary Islands. Every time we arrived at an island, we went out and greeted people welcomed them to come on board Elida.
Remembering when we arrived at Hönö, then we had received a message one day earlier that the whole crew was welcome to eat Christmas smorgasbord. Tarren knew nothing about this man, but the entire crew left the boat and went up to the hotel, the owner and his wife stood on the stairs and welcomed us all. Then they led us to a special room, which was set up and prepared. No one knew anything about this, but we were curious. He asked us to sit down, which we all did. Then he stood up with his wife and told us why he invited us. "We heard the songs and the message from your boat in the summer, when you sailed by, I have received the message of Jesus in my heart, and it has changed me. I no longer have any interest in serving alcohol in the hotel, only if someone orders food, I can help with alcohol with food alone. I am so grateful for what you do and for the experience I have received. Therefore, I want to invite you all to a smorgasbord. Please be my guests now!

Conference in Halmstad

I went to a Christian conference in Halmstad with Kjell, my brother in law. Miriam and Kjell had moved back to Sweden and lived in Trollhättan. At the meeting, we got to meet Gösta Öman, who was a preacher and a missionary who had moved back from South Korea, when his wife died. We became acquainted and talked about attending the (FGBMFI) World Conference in Melbourne 1985.

More sad news

My cousin Tore was ill and was at Vänersborg's hospital over Christmas, then Kjell and I went there, we brought with us the tape recorder where we had beautiful Christian music. We asked Tore if we could play a little for him. He gladly said, yes. After playing several songs, he asked us to play the first song again. After a few days, in early January 1985, my cousin Tore died. Furthermore, we received another death message. Dad's brother Georg had also died, and we went to his funeral just outside Trollhättan.
What a massive year this was, we were very stunned, from one sorrow to the other. Now it was time to return to Australia.

The van is on fire

I trained another salesman, and we packed the van for a trip up to Queensland. This trip went north over the coast of NSW and QLD to Townsville, and then we turned straight east towards MT. Isa and down to

Charlieville, it was late afternoon, and then I used to always go to the next town so that we can start at 9 am when the shops open. Just before Roma, a kangaroo jumped out on the road, right in front of the van, I didn't have any chance to avoid an accident, but hit the kangaroo. I stopped and checked in front of the truck, but the damage was not significant, so we drove on. I soon noticed that it started to smell smoke in the van and stopped and checked inside in front of the feet. It flashed a little bit there, and smoke came up. Then I saw that the electrical cables were peeled off when the bonnet was pushed in, and insulation around the wires was damaged because they were stretched when the plate was pushing them inwards. I couldn't access the cables. A truck stopped, and I asked for a crowbar, with the driver, but he did not have one. We got out and started to unload the prints on the grass at the roadside, plus our bags. The van had now started to burn, the tank was full of diesel, but nothing happened, the van just burned down. Then we noticed that the grass began to burn, we could only get hold of four prints plus our bags, the rest of our stock burned up. The fire brigade arrived, and it was late in the evening. They couldn't save the van, and it was too late.

We noticed that one of the firefighters had one large boot and one small boot, I asked why. Then he replied a little embarrassed that he slept when the alarm went off and he just pulled on the boots in the dark without checking that they were of equal size. The police came and gave us a ride to Roma. He gave me a tip for the next time I would run over a kangaroo, to aim at the centre of the vehicle, where the bull bar is most durable. We stayed overnight in Roma and went bus back to Sydney the next day.

Bought Toyota Coaster bus

Curt is showing one of the pictures we were selling

We needed to buy a larger vehicle, the small vans were not big enough, and we always had many orders back with us to Sydney after each sales trip. Which meant a lot of extra work of packing orders, and also transport companies damaged many prints. We used to deliver directly to the customer, and then we got paid directly. A larger vehicle would mean that we could make longer trips and still have enough stock with us. We could also go with two vans, one big and one small, then the small van, "refill" with more stock along the roads.

I went down to a car salesman who only sold trucks and buses at Princes Hwy in Arncliffe. There I saw a Toyota Coaster bus that had been a rental bus that Budget rent a car had used. It had a 3.4-litre diesel engine. It was full of dents both inside and out, and it had lots of scratches on it. You could say that it looked like "seven difficult years". But it only cost $10,000. Which was cheap, we used to pay about $18,000 for a new but a much smaller van. This one had 24 seats and was 6 metres long, and the height was about 2,7 metres. I was going to remove at least 20 seats in it, and install metal shelves, and a bed across the back so that I could sleep during the long journeys. I asked Irmeli to meet me at the dealer and have a look at it, and I thought she would not want such a big bus with all those flaws. But when she saw the bus she said, it is excellent. She said she understood that it had good potential and capacity. I drove it down to a small smash repair shop at Taren Point and asked for a quote, to repair the bus. I told him jokingly that this one keeps you busy on a Saturday afternoon. He walked around the bus and said it would cost $1900. Then he would also do it inside out. Okay, I said. It was a very low price for an excellent job. When it was ready, I went up to my insurance company NRMA to get it valued. They valued it at $18,000. It looked like new, with original decals (Toyota Coaster) on it as well.

Irmeli and I went on a trip to Adelaide and back another way to Sydney. I had checked in at a campsite in Adelaide, waiting for Irmeli to come from Broken Hill, but Irmeli was very late. It was on July 15th, and we were going to celebrate my birthday. I was waiting along the roadside in the evening edge, and there came Irmeli! First I gave her a kiss and a hug, then she walked around the van and opened the hatch in the back, very proudly and showed me it was only one single print laying on the floor. What has happened?

Then she happily told me that in Broken Hill, she had gone to a new store that had just opened. The owner was interested and asked her to bring in some prints, she looked at them but said nothing, but asked if Irmeli had more prints. Irmeli carried in several prints, and she looked at them again, said nothing but asked for more. Irmeli tried to make a trial close to finding out if the owner was interested in buying them, but the owner just said, do you have more prints. In the end, Irmeli had carried the entire van's stock apart from one painting that was a duplicate. Then the owner said, "write them down". Irmeli was so happy, hardly believed her blessing. It was a new gift shop which celebrated the opening with champagne, the owner poured up a glass to Irmeli, but when she went back into the shop Irmeli quickly poured out the champagne in the sink, when the owner came in, she said, "oh have you already drunk it up, then I will pour you up some more". But Irmeli declined this time. Irmeli had finished completing the invoice, and the lady gave her the cheque.

Toyota Coaster Bus was stolen.

But the Toyota Coaster bus didn't last long before it was stolen on Boxing day, on the street outside our apartment. I went out on the balcony at Boxing Day and noticed that something was missing. After a while, I noticed that my Toyota Coaster bus was not there. I ran out and double-checked up and down the street, but it was gone. I reported this to the police, and the police started to work on getting hold of the thieves. However, a customer called from the sunshine coast north of Brisbane and wanted to buy the oval pictures for $5.

We said we have no such prints. Then he said it was a stamp with our company name behind the board. I told only the print itself costs more than $5. I asked where he bought them, and he said someone came in and sold them to him. I told them that we had our bus stolen, including the prints. But at least he ordered the pictures of me at regular prices. The insurance company paid out part of the loss, and also the cost of the vehicle. The police arrested those who sold the prints and tracked the warehouse, and then we were offered to repurchase them if we wanted, which we did not. These prints were cast with a thick lacquer in a factory in Sydney, and they were called decoupage prints. When one of the workers in the factory took a smoke break, the factory exploded in flames, whereby the worker died. The factory was sold to another company, with which we continued to do business.

Satan worshippers found

Irmeli was on a business trip in northern NSW and came to Coonabarabran when she asked a customer about the nearest way to go to the next town. He explained that there was a shorter route, and explained that she should choose the left fork in a forest crossing. He said DON'T yield to the right. But she turned to the right and entered a narrow forest road, winded up being a dead end, which led to open space inside the forest. There were a lot of people dressed in black and had high black conical hats. A crying mother was sitting next to an altar where her baby laid and would be sacrificed. Irmeli stepped out of the van and with firm steps in holy anger, came to the mother and took the child and mother and the man, back to her van, and returned to the right crossing this time. They must have seen the registration number of the truck because afterwards, we got many strange conversations and death threats for several years.

One night, several weeks after the incident, we smelled smoke in our apartment, then I opened the door, and saw that it was burning outside our door. The fire burned slowly because of the fireproof door and hallway carpet. We called the police.
The next trip I was up in Queensland, when I received a strange phone call, he said he wanted to come down to the store and buy. I answered, "No one was there now, but I will come down", and I didn't want to say that I was far away.

My cousin Lasse and Ulla and Camilla's cousin Anneli had come to visit us just before Christmas, and they were told what had happened. Lasse could only see on one eye, and he said that he would stand fire guard all night with a thick wooden stick in his hand and look through the peep-hole in the door. Lasse was very determined and guarded all night, but nothing happened that night. Another night it burned again, but this time the fire was on top of the stairs. The police were given a lead to a neighbour on the next floor, but that did not lead anywhere. That neighbour was a bit odd and strange, but not suspected any more for causing the fires.

There was also a 10-year-old boy who had called us for three years and left cheeky messages on our answering machine when we were not at home. But in the end, the police tracked him to a fixed address and handed over everything to us. We went there to the family and talked to them, the boy admitted to the parents and us and apologised, at last, we had peace at home.

Limited Edition by Kevin Best

Kevin Best was a very well known artist in Australia, and his art was characterised by "A Brush with light" this is displayed in all of his landscape paintings. We went to see him in Sydney's Northern Suburbs and asked him if he could paint a story, similar to McCubbin "the Pioneers". Which was a very popular print. He said that he already had one such painting and would paint another three paintings with a narrative theme titled "A Family Affair". We made a series of four prints of those paintings. Where this family were camping in the bush, gathering firewood and pitched a tent, a child having a pony ride, and fishing at the river. We made a contract with Kevin Best for him to sign all those 750 limited edition prints, by personal signature. We sold a few hundred of them, but still today we have some left in stock, for anyone to buy. Those prints are now a collector's item. Kevin Best died 31st July 2012.

A Family Affair, by Kevin Best copyright Cultura 1996

A Good Cast

Camping with Nana and Pop

Getting the Firewood

The Young Riders

We signed a contract with Kevin Best, for the copyright of "A Family Affair".

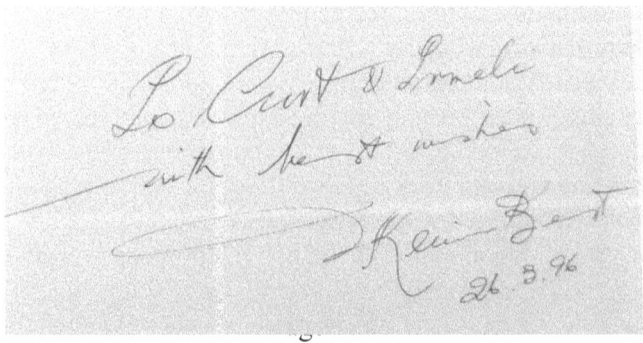

Limited editions of d'Arcy Doyle

Man From Snowy River 2, limited edition

You may view our different prints at www.australianlimitededitionprints.com

We also printed limited edition prints by Lawrence Starkey, who is a very skilful artist, his paintings are full of details, and he paints excellent portraits of American Indians, but also landscapes with campfires in a mountainous area of US, which we also have in stock.

Ministering Bibles into Russia

We came to Sweden during the last year of the Soviet Union era, when Mikhail Gorbachev was president. When we were going back to Australia, we flew over the Soviet Union, with a stopover in Moscow. We decided to bring some bibles and children clothing with us. We had friends in Moscow, from an earlier trip. I think their name was something like Cherkaskey, he was a former military officer in the Russian army, and his wife was the leader of the Red Cross in Russia. I had shared the gospel with him earlier and also left him with a new testament, that Pro Hart, a very famous Australian artist, had painted a flower onto the back cover.

We had just left Sweden and were at the international airport in Moscow. I put my suitcase on the baggage belt for scanning, but I must have been nervous and put the suitcase with all the bibles in, the wrong way across the belt, that made the security officer mad and shouted to me, to take my bag and walk out. Praise the Lord, with all the bibles.

This time we went to visit a Russian family who was Christians and the father was a pastor. We took a suburban train to the Russian family, pressed the doorbell. And an elderly lady opened up a little, and then she flung the door open and asked us to come in. After greeting the family, we gave them the bibles and the children's clothing. The husband told us about their persecution. KGB visited him, and they thought that he was a spy, and he was charged for spying and got sentenced to jail for five years, but in court, the judge asked him if after he received his sentence if he would have anything he wishes to say. He just thanked God, and blessed Russia, the judge got mad, and immediately changed his sentence to 10 years instead of just the five years. After that, he had served five years in jail, the revolution came, and Mikhail Gorbachev came to power. The authorities then didn't know what to do with him, so they sent him home. He said to us that he is so thankful for Russia.

Gold Coast with Anneli

I packed the car with framed "limited edition prints" they were signed by the artist and only produced in a limit number. They were more expensive than other prints, and many bought them as an investment. I had a customer in Glen Innes who sold used furniture, but also prints. Everything in his shop was very cheap except those prints that he had bought from another company. I stopped in Glen Innes, where our customer was situated. I carried two limited edition prints he said nothing but wanted to see more prints, I brought in another two prints, and he said nothing but asked only to see more. He came out to the car to check if I didn't have more prints, and wanted to buy the last one, but I told him — unfortunately, it for a customer on the Gold Coast. We went in again, and I wondered if I would carry out all my prints back since he had not shown any purchasing interest except to look at the prints. Some customers are such that they want to look and buy nothing. Now the customer said, write an invoice for all the pictures. Thanks, I said and gave him my invoice, and he paid me with a cheque. I went to the Gold Coast with only one print with Irmeli and Anneli, and there we got to spend the remaining days on leisure.

The hiring of a new salesman

We needed additional salespeople, then a young man called Robert came who was Swedish. We knew his mother and father well, and they were terrific friends with us. He went up by train from Wollongong, and I met him at the station in Allawah. When I saw him, God showed me that it is a new son to me. And he was called Robert. He had to start in the warehouse and pack orders, to learn the products, and what was selling well. Irmeli trained him after his time in the store as a salesman. He had no experience as a salesman, but he became an excellent and very friendly salesman who produced excellent results. Robert had two friends who also wanted jobs, Peter and David. I asked Peter to come to the office. After the interview, it became clear that Peter would start in the warehouse before he would sell, to learn all the products. Peter's father was from Scotland but had died, and Peter missed his father very much. Peter asked me if he could call me father, I said, yes. After a month, Peter wanted to sell, and I said he had to wait another month.

But then I took him with me out to sell in Queensland, we went up to Cairns and then the coast down, we came to Mackay it was after 5 PM, and I wanted to drive the 330 km to Rockhampton so we could start selling there the next day. We stopped briefly at the city border, so Peter could make a bedside for him to sleep in the van while I planned on continuing to drive. Peter left the door open, and a lot of mosquitoes came in, then I asked Peter to close the door, which he did. After a while, I asked him if he was ready so that I could drive. OK, Peter said. I resumed driving while Peter had fallen asleep in the rear of the vehicle. After half the way I stopped, and we changed over. We arrived in Rockhampton before 9 PM, and we went to a restaurant to eat supper. I used always to call Irmeli and report every day, which I also did now. She responded with such a long sigh and began to thank God that I lived. She said that a woman had called her up and found my order portfolio alongside the road. There were all my cheques and orders. The company name and the phone number were on all the company orders. Then Irmeli feared that I had been murdered. This long stretch between Mackay and Rockhampton is notorious for robbery and the like because it is just forest and no settlement. After the conversation, I asked Peter who sat and ate, where is my order portfolio? He looked up and thought, then he covered his eyes, and said "I put it outside the van when I was making my bed in the van at Mackay", then I said that the briefcase had been found by a lady, who would post it to Irmeli! Peter immediately became much calmer.

Peter became an excellent salesman. Now I have to have a new man at the warehouse, and then his brother David got to work with us. David was a quiet and shy man, but worked very well! We tried to encourage David that he should also sell, I brought him with me a couple of times, but after I let him continue to work in the warehouse, and cash sales in the shop. Once a customer came into the store and had a look. David served this customer and was so encouraged that the customer bought a painting. Afterwards, David told us, "It was certainly my charm that gave him sale". David had gained greater confidence with our encouragement. We now had two people in the office, besides me and Irmeli and Camilla. We were all Christians and had a great time together. It was joy daily.

Peter was an excellent salesman, and we received feedback from one of our customers in Queensland, who asked me why they cannot buy more from Cultura. I wondered why. Then they said that Peter had been with them and showed oil paintings, but he wanted to sell three boxes of paintings. Three different sizes with six paintings in each box. They just wanted to buy one box. Then Peter said I might come back to you, but I want to see if I can sell all three boxes to someone first. And Peter never came back. He always sold the whole package deal to the customers and became an excellent salesman. He also had a girlfriend with whom he was in love.

When Robert made his first trip alone as a salesman, he told me that when he came to his first customer, Robert sat for 20 minutes in the van and hesitated if he would go in. Finally, he went in. Robert was a charming salesman and had a very soft and honest presentation of our products. A few years later he studied part-time, to become a real estate salesman, while still selling prints. He later resigned, and became a very successful real estate salesman!

Bloodbath in Mt. Isa

Irmeli and I were on a business trip to Darwin, and we were stopping in Mt. Isa to sell before embarking to the 1600 km long journey to Darwin. We were looking for a motel, and it was difficult to find any accommodation this time in Mt. Isa. It was not unusual, because sometimes the different towns have their shows or similar attractions, and most people in the surrounding areas take the opportunity to "go into town". However, at last, we found a motel and went in to check in. We felt the people working at the reception were very strange. But this was our only choice of accommodation, so we booked the only available room that was left. It was in the afternoon, so we just left our bags in the room, and went down to the centre to get something to eat. After we had our meal, I said to Irmeli, that I have a witness in my spirit that something terrible was going to happen tonight. I asked her if I should go to the police. But on second thought, I thought that the police was not going to believe me. So I did not do anything about my revelation.

When we came back to the motel, a lady came into our room, and asked Irmeli, "can I do yours". Irmeli answered her kindly, "do yours, and I do mine". Then the lady went out of our room. It was time to sleep, and I barricaded the door with our chair. At about 1 AM, we woke up, and Irmeli wanted to go to the toilet. I opened the door, and the lights were on the outside, and an ambulance was there and the police. It was blood everywhere. The cops asked Irmeli where she was going. She said to the toilet. Police said, be very careful because we have not caught the perpetrator yet. When Irmeli opened the door to the bathroom and closed it behind her, she suddenly discovered the perpetrator sitting on the floor with a bloody knife in his hands. Irmeli screamed. When police kicked up the door, Irmeli fell over the man, but the blade passed between her arm and her body, miraculously not piercing her.

Journey with Kjell to Darwin

Kjell was currently unemployed, and I asked if he wanted to come with me to Darwin on a business trip. We then went via Broken Hill, Port Augusta, Coober Pedy where there were opal mines, and Alice Springs, Tennant Creek, Darwin, Mt. Isa, Longreach, Charleville, Rome, Toowoomba and New England Highway to Sydney. On such long journeys, I do not take with me so much cash, due to the theft risk, I just brought the cheque book, but I can only pay the hotels with it. Everyone does not accept business cheques. Therefore it is necessary to have the cash to pay for food, petrol and the like.

We loaded our trailer and started our journey. Kjell is a good driver, and he usually drives large buses with school children. When we were in Coober Pedy and were driving towards Alice Springs, Kjell took the first pass, and it was a journey of 680 km. We started the trip in the afternoon and would change drivers when either of us got tired. I laid myself in the back of the van. We had sold so many prints now that there was plenty of space. I lay with my head against the tailgate and the shelf was about 90 cm over me so that I couldn't close the door from the inside. Kjell had to shut the door. I fell asleep but woke up of that the van started to shake very much, I shouted at Kjell, but he did not answer, I screamed and shouted at Kjell but still no answer. Finally, the van stopped with a jerk. Then Kjell answered, and opened the door for me. Kjell told me that he had fallen asleep at the steering wheel. He crossed the road on the left, and turned right across the road, to the other side, and finally stopped in front of a small tree. I went out and looked, there was damage to the trailer, but the van seemed OK. It was now in the middle of the night, in the middle of the desert, the centre of Australia. From there, I continued to drive while Kjell got a much-needed rest.

The next day we sold in Alice Springs and continued towards Tennant Creek and then to Katherine. But we stopped at a hot spring and bathed, located 140 km south-east of Katherine or 440 km south-east of Darwin, Kjell enjoyed this very much. And then we sold in Katherine. There were many aborigines there, that received grants and did not work, and had fallen for alcohol. They used to sleep out in the open, but they had gotten new homes, which many did not like, and some of them pulled out the beds and slept outside. Now it was just 310 km to Darwin.

We got there on Saturday afternoon, and Kjell told me he was craving for a paw. We went to church the next day on Sunday, after the service, we met an older man in the church, he said he had brought two pawpaw's, but did not know why the man did it, it was just to one man he would give a paw paw. He asked Kjell if he

wanted a paw paw. Kjell thanked him very much.
On Monday we went from Darwin to Mt. Isa, it's a journey of 1600 km, with just Katherine in between, rest is the only desert. There is no speed limit in the Northern Territory, but we cannot drive more than 80 km/h because otherwise, the trailer will start to roll. We heard of a Japanese tourist who drove at very high speed there, and he hit an animal and crashed his car.

From Mt. Isa, we turned south, and when we got to Roma, I had run out of cash. The problem was that I couldn't go to the bank and redeem my cheque because they had to call my bank in Sydney and fax my signature and wait for an answer. In the morning, I showed Kjell my empty wallet and said that I had run out of cash, but God will give us money. It usually happens sometimes that the customer pays cash for their prints, but it is not so common. Now I needed money, and God will bless us today with cash. The first customer I visited, bought pictures and should pay, but I would not help God to ask for cash, it was Kjell who should see what God is doing. The customer said to me "I have to pay you with cash". Then I said loudly "praise the Lord". She asked why I said that when I told her my situation. She said, I don't know, but I have to pay you with cash anyway. The trip to Sydney was just 1050 km.

Outi returns to Sweden.

Outi wanted to go back to Sweden, and Irmeli accompanied her and kept her company. Sirpa and Kaj had arranged a furnished flat for her. And the dinner was ready when she got there from the airport. She started going to the Finnish church in Eskilstuna. Irmeli took a temporary job as an interpreter. Irmeli could speak fluent Finnish and Swedish.

Ministering

Mission trip to the Philippines

Gösta Öman whom I met in Halmstad in Sweden, had invited us to go with him to the Philippines on a mission trip, which we gladly accepted.
I flew with Camilla from Sydney to Manilla, and Irmeli flew from Sweden, and we met at the airport in Manila. I met John from Melbourne, who was in the team, and his wife Birgit had become an agent for our products in Melbourne. Mark from Australia was also in our group. It was an exciting experience.

We stayed in Meycauayan for a few days. There, Gösta would preach in a church. After the sermon, Gösta asked for those who wanted prayer to come forward. Irmeli and the others of the team stood at the front, ready to pray for those who came forward. Then a man took a few steps in the direction of Irmeli, then all of a sudden he was thrown down to the floor by an invisible force and shouted and made strange sounds. He laid on the floor, and I wondered in my heart, "where did she learn all this?" She prayed for him, and he became calm. Afterwards, I understood that it was the presence of Jesus that caused the spirit within that man to manifest. Irmeli had not learned anything but only read the Bible. Early in the morning hours, we heard someone walking around praying and confessing Bible texts. He was a Christian but a former Jehovah's Witnesses. Per-Inge participated in this trip, and became a self-appointed travel leader, and kept excellent order of us.

The journey now went up to Bambang in Nueva Vizcaya province. It would be a pastor conference for pastors across the Philippines. Everyone got to sleep in the church, and the host couple moved into a wardrobe. But we had a great time with a lot of love and joy. Gösta preached in the evenings, and there were many miracles and signs. I had the privilege of standing next to Gösta when he preached, so I could easily film what was happening, which was precisely what Gösta wanted. Every night we returned to where we lived, I checked through the video. But oh, what a lot of people were behind me who wanted to see the video. We had to borrow a TV so everyone could see better. Then we went to a town called Aritao, there was a small group of girls with us, and including Camilla, they sang on the bus and at the meetings. Gösta preached in the evening, and there were not so many who came.

After the sermon, the team began praying for all those who wanted prayer, and there were many. There was a boy about an 8-10-year-old boy who was completely deaf, standing very near the platform where I was standing with my camera. I had him right in focus with my camera. During the prayer, one of the team members gave him a watch to listen. He nodded frantically that he could hear. A deaf boy got his hearing. The town of Aritao had a population of 37,000. And many knew about this deaf boy. I was out in town and asked people to come to this meeting, e.g. a man on the bus I talked to, he wanted to come, but said he didn't have the money. I said he could get money from me, but only if he went to the meeting. Yes, he said, he would come.

The next night we went there again, it was a lot of people there. The deaf boy who was miraculously healed had made a difference. I had set up my camera on the big platform, and then a man came towards me, it was the man from the bus. I recognised him, and he wanted to sit on the chairs on the platform, he thought he was the guest of honour. But I couldn't speak the language, and let him sit down on the platform. The meeting started, and Gösta preached very well, it became great response, many wanted prayer, at the end that man came again to me, I asked if he received prayer, he said yes. Then I asked him if he received healing. Of course, he said, for him it was obvious. Bible says that God has chosen the poor in this world RICH in faith. Faith is their wealth.

Irmeli had disappeared one day from where we lived, but she came back in the middle of the day. She told me that she had been in a hospital and asked if she could visit someone sick. The doctor showed her to a man who had tuberculosis. She talked to him and asked if she could pray for him in the name of Jesus. He was grateful for that, and she prayed for him. She asked me if I wanted to go to the hospital. We went there, and when we got into where the man was, he sat up in bed and seemed alert. We asked how he felt, he said very well. We left him there but gave our address in Australia to him so that he could write to us. He wrote a letter to us after three months and confirmed his healing.

We visited a Swedish couple, Dennis and Inga-Lill, who had gone there as missionaries with their son.

They had come to the Philippines with nothing and had now started daycare centres, plus a school and a church. A private person and supported their ministry. The school was for children in slum areas. The parents who could not afford to pay the fees were sponsored by other people, while others could afford to pay the costs for the school.

We had a church service in Bambang. The church was packed, with a lot of people, including many children and babies. I had my camera as usual at the front, so I had all the visitors in focus. During the sermon, a baby became hungry, then the mother just fully exposed her breast to feed her baby. She was sitting right in front of me, and I couldn't avoid her. It was our first missionary journey, and it was terrific in every way. The people are so receptive to God's Word, poor but happy.

Importing oil paintings from China

After Christmas 1989, sales started rolling as usual. We needed to get our motifs painted, and we wanted to go to Hong Kong to search for suppliers. We also wanted to smuggle Bibles into China. We had a contact in Hong Kong who would provide us with packed bags of various Christian literature. I wrestled a little with the thought if this was legal and asked God about it. I was given the word, "Man shall not live by bread alone, but by every word that proceedeth out of the mouth of God". Then I thought that is the Word of God, and then it is not just some nationalities that will live off that bread, but all nations have equal rights to the Word of God. Then I got peace. There would be two trips to China. The time for departure approached, we wanted our church to pray for us. We had never done anything like this before. We had a visiting preacher named Samuel Doctorian, he laid his hands on us together with our pastor Norman Armstrong and prayed. Samuel Doctorian gave a word prophecy to us that said, "The enemy will try to stop you, but if you hold on to your faith in Jesus, you will succeed".

Then Camilla, Irmeli and I, flew to Hong Kong. We

visited some suppliers for oil paintings, they insisted we would have lunch with them, which we did, and it was a 10-course lunch. Then we visited another company who also insisted on having lunch with us in the afternoon, we said we were not hungry, but they asked again, and we had to give in to their request, and go out and eat a 10-course lunch for the same day. The next day we went out in the afternoon so that you didn't get double meal again.

Bible smuggling to Xiamen

The first smuggle trip with the Bibles was to Xiamen north of Hong Kong on the coast. We went to a church there; afterwards, an older Chinese couple invited us for lunch. They were so lovely and hospitable. We had not yet met our contact who would take the bibles. Back to the hotel, somebody called at our door. There was our contact, who was a westerner. He said we were going for a walk and carrying the bags around the shoulder when we went together. Then we parted after a while. He went on with the bag on his shoulder. Then we went back to Hong Kong.

Bible smuggling to Guangzhou I

The next trip into China was to Guangzhou by train from Hong Kong. We had one bag, each with Bibles and Christian literature. We went off the train at Guangzhou, and it was a lot of people on the platform. We saw two doors on the wall in front of us. We went toward the right door, and as I was going to enter through the door, Irmeli pushed me aside and went in first. Irmeli filled out a document and continued to walk straight through the custom, and we were told to ignore the security officers. But they called on her to come back. She then was asked to leave her bag on the belt, so her bag could be scanned. The security officer took the bag after it was examined, and started to ask her questions. He asked, "what is inside your bag"? God said to her, tell the truth. So she said, "bibles". He then lifted the bag and said, "it is heavy". Irmeli said, "it is not enough". He asked her, "why do you do this"? Irmeli said, "because I love Jesus". He started to become nervous now, and went back and forth and took off his cap and hit himself at the chest with it while pacing back and forth. Then he came back to Irmeli and asked, "give me the key to the lock". Irmeli said, "my husband has the key".

While all this happened to Irmeli, I walked through the customs in the same manner as Irmeli, and they called me to come back, I pretended not to hear them, and then I felt someone touching my shoulder, I looked around and saw the security officer and he showed me to come back and put my bag on the belt. I waited on the other side of the belt for my bag to arrive. It appeared to take a long time because I was in suspense. At last, my bag came, and no one said anything. I was surprised since my bag was full of bibles, and they especially asked me to go back. Probably an angel blocked their eyes, that they did not see the bibles.

Camilla was next in turn, she proceeded the same way as me, ignoring the security officers, and was pulled up, and have to come back to the belt for her bags to be scanned. She had a rug sack on her back where her bibles were, and also she had cabin baggage with all her clothing, where she did not have any bibles. She only put her bag on the belt. And it came through, but nobody noticed her rug sack on her back. She came out to me outside the railway station, and I said to her, come quickly now, we take a taxi to the hotel. She said, "no, I won't leave mum there inside". I told her, "come on". But she refused to come, so we had to wait for Irmeli to come out. Shortly Irmeli came with her bag of bibles happily. And we took the taxi together to the hotel — no more incidents.

Bible smuggling to Guangzhou II

We went to Macau with a flying boat that went on an airbag, with Boeing engines. It was a smooth boat trip. We were visiting a silk flower company in Macau. We ordered a container, including a fantasy design of a flower that I thought of myself. Black stems with pink flowers. They wanted to invite us to lunch again, and it became such a great lunch. Irmeli ate snake, and something else weird. I adhered to what I knew. We brought the bible bags with us and would now go by taxi to Guangzhou. It took almost half a day, and finally, we went after sunset. It was very dark, and hard to see all the people on the road. They save electricity in China, so it is very dark at night. We arrived without accidents to Guangzhou and checked into a four-star hotel, and it had a sizeable three-storey waterfall within the hotel. We left our bags at the reception and received a receipt.

We looked a little at the city, the meat market was under open sky, and in a warm climate, there was a dead dog in a corner, and they also had chickens and hens, there was someone who wanted to buy a chicken thigh, then they took a live chicken and chopped off that thigh. The chicken then jumped around with one leg. It is pure animal torture, horrible. Many other animal tortures are going on, and I do not want to mention here. We got enough of China this time, so we went back to Australia.

Bible smuggling to Shanghai

We had received some flying reward points, which we wanted to use. We were allowed to fly anywhere in Asia, and also a free side trip. We choose Japan, with a free side trip to Shanghai, everything in first class. We were allowed 120 kg of baggage. We told the office in Hong Kong that we wanted to smuggle Bibles into Shanghai. They told us that it is impossible because everyone who enters with bibles will be caught. We said that we still wanted to go. They would arrange with our bibles. This time Irmeli couldn't carry any bags, so I had to give all of them. We had 115 kg of baggage, and I think we had four suitcases. I had to take two bags at a time, while Irmeli was waiting in one end, and no one looked after the other two bags, and no one stole them.

We came to Shanghai and waited for our bags at the baggage belt. We waited until some more people came, but very few came. We looked suspicious if we were waiting for too long, so we headed for the way out, where a security officer stood. Then another couple squeezed in before us, and they were caught by the security officer. So we just went straight through. We came to the hotel and waited for one man to go and pick up the bibles, but no one arrived. I had a contact number in Shanghai whom I contacted at his work. But he was not available. So I had to call Hong Kong, which was very dangerous. It was a swift call. They were going to solve this problem. After some time, someone knocked on our door. I went to open and was pushed back by two men, they went straight to the TV, and sat down in front of the TV signalling to me to come.

They said that the room was bugged, and we could only talk in front of the TV. We agreed to go down to reception where our bags were, and I gave them the two bags with bibles. They took the two bags, and we took two taxis, and they went to one taxi and Irmeli and me in the other cab. We followed their taxi for a couple of kilometres, then we split up, and they went a different way from us.

Back to business

The silk flowers come.

We placed our order of silk flowers. It was a popular uprising in China in 1989 in June that caused this delay. Then we were told about the massacre in Tiananmen Square. A month later, our silk flowers came.

Birgit got her samples and order blocks in the autumn of 1989 to be able to go out and sell silk flowers. She sold well and sent orders regularly to us. Irmeli worked in the office now and had to steer the company up because we had more staff and more orders come in.

It was also soon time for us to celebrate our 25th wedding anniversary, on the South Sea Islands. Irmeli was busy packing the last orders of silk flowers alone in the company while I was at home. She got up on a very tall ladder that was over 2 metres high, and fetched flowers from the storage shelves, when she would descend from the ladder, she miscalculated her step and thought she would be standing on the floor with the next pace down from the ladder, when in fact there were two more rungs left. Thou she didn't lose balance and fell over, the fall due to miscalculation caused a severe internal injury to her right hip socket. The impaction was fatal. It hurt, but she didn't breathe a word about her accident to me, fearing she'd lose out on going overseas to celebrate our 25th wedding anniversary. She secretly hoped her pain would dissolve, but we went to the Cook Islands.

This island belongs to New Zealand, and they speak English there. The whole island is Christian, but in spite of this, they preach the gospel in the square every week, with a great choir. We went to the old great white stone church on Sunday to listen to the sermon. You could even read in the tourist brochure about, "Don't forget to go to church". We understood why, when we came to church. The worship in the church before the service was somewhat heavenly. Everyone sat down on the benches mixed with a lot of tourists. Then women began to sing all over the place; all of them sat mixed among all the tourists. Then the men also began to tune into the song of praise.

No singing from the front, just out in the congregation. No choir leader. They sang with such harmony that it is difficult to describe; one would need to experience it themselves. That's why it was in the tourist brochure. We flew from there to Western Samoa and stayed at the Tusitala Hotel in Apia. One morning Irmeli couldn't get out of bed, she said she had a lot of pain in her hip. Then I got to know the truth about her accident at the company. We went to the hospital, where she obtained an injection, which relieved the intensity of the pain somewhat.

Irmeli suffered very much pain throughout the years since her first hip operation in Australia. Unfortunately, she got an infection in the right hip from the first hip operation in Australia. The surgeon came into the operation theatre to check on the air conditioning prior to see if the temperature was cold enough. Then he operated Irmeli. That operation was not functional, and she started to feel a lot of pain very early. And the result was that after about two years, she needed another surgery. But we did not want the same surgeon. We got the best surgeon this time who had excellent recommendations. When that surgeon operated Irmeli, he asked for a prosthetics, but unfortunately, they only had a long one in stock. And that made Irmeli's leg 7 cm longer than the other. She had to have a built-up shoe. She continued to have a lot of pain, and she also had an infection in the hip. We sought medical advice from another surgeon, and he said that another operation could be fatal, at worst.

We did not want to take that risk and started to investigate the possibilities for Irmeli to be operated in the USA. But it seemed to be very complicated, by insurance etc. And how I should make a living there. Then we contacted some of our friends in Sweden, who were working in hospitals. They said that Sweden is outstanding in hip replacements, as a matter of fact, when we checked it out, Sweden is leading in orthopaedic surgery in the world, followed by Finland and Norway, the USA was on the fourth place. Finally, we found a doctor at Sahlgrenska in Gothenburg, Sweden. He was an expert on revisions of total hip arthroplasties. I e-mailed an X-ray to him and called him and asked for his medical opinion. He said it is a good chance of success. Which resulted in that we planned to go to Sweden for a hip operation in 2000. Unfortunately, over time, there were a total of 9 surgeries, due to infections, none of which granted any improvements or full functionality.

The vicar comes

In early August my friend Otto visited us from Sweden, he was a vicar and had a few weeks off. I had arranged to make an extended trip to Cairns in Queensland and then back via Mt. Isa, Charlieville, Rome and Sydney travelling a total distance of 8000 km. Otto had preached to King Carl-Gustaf and Silvia of Sweden and had a photo with him of the king and queen and himself. He told every customer about this and gave them a picture. Otto also liked sailing, so I let him off at the coast of Bowen and drove around in the cities and came back in the afternoon and picked him up. Also, in Mt. Morgan, I made Otto go down and have a look at the mine, while I was selling. We went right up to Cairns and Green Island to turn down to Townsville and towards Cloncurry where Otto preached in a church in the evening.

We took the usual route south via Winton and Charlieville and then Brisbane. We stopped and refuelled at a large petrol station in southern Brisbane, and it was time to rearrange a little in the van for the 900 km journey to Sydney. After I had paid at the station, I sat down in the truck and drove away. After we had driven quite a few km, Otto discovered that my portfolio was not in the van. He said it was left on the ground at the petrol station. I said it did not matter, and we prayed a simple prayer together that God would send the bag to me. It was a petrol station where many tourist buses stopped. So there was no point in going back. Once at the office in Sydney, the phone rang from the Greyhound Bus company. They asked me if my

name was Curt Larsson and if the company was called
Cultura Pty Ltd, I answered yes it was. They had a bag
there with cheques in. They said their bus driver
thought it had to belong to one of their passengers, so
he took it to Sydney. Thank God, we got it, all my work
and money were in it.

Travel to Sweden and Finland

I would now go on a sales trip to Sweden and Finland. I
wanted to increase sales of the unique Australian prints,
with Australian leather printed with a velvet-like motif.
In Sweden, I bought a used Fiat for 3000 kronor, which
I drove within Sweden and Finland. But when I came to
Västerås, something happened to the car, it stopped, but
it happened outside the Fiat workshop. God is good.
There was a problem with the petrol pump, which only
cost a few dollars, and it was fixed. In Stockholm,
orders were received from Åhlens and another small
company in Sweden. After that, I went to Finland, and
there it became much slower, so I spent time with
Jouko who had moved back to Finland. He was about
to move from Helsinki to Mäntsälä about 50 kilometres
north of Helsinki. It was a lot of work with his move
and the time for my ferry in Naantali was approaching,
It crossed my mind that I needed to call and book a
place, I would have to bring the car with me on the
ship. But I forgot all about this and said goodbye, and
was off to Naantali. When I was on my way towards
Naantali I remembered that I had not booked a place,
but then it was too late, the smartphone was not
discovered at that time. I arrived in Naantali, where the
ferry site is, I had to wait in a separate queue, in case

there was space available on the ferry. Many cars that went on the ship and it seemed to be quite full. In the end, there were some places left, and my queue began to move forward. I got on to the ferry as the last car. Once inside the boat, I was allocated a part in a 4-berth cabin.

When I got into the cabin, I greeted the three guys and started unpacking my bag. Then I heard a voice that seemed familiar to me, and I pretended to look for something in my bag, while I was frantically thinking about where I had heard this voice before. Suddenly I remembered and turned around and pointed to the man who was lying at the bottom of the other bunk bed and I said "Otto", and he said "Sydney". We went up on deck and sat in the restaurant, and he told us that on Monday he used to go ferry to Åland, on his day off as a priest. Then he went off the boat and prayed to God in the park. But this time, when the ferry arrived in Åland, he changed his mind and went on to Naantali. But he did not know that they did not accept Swedish credit cards in Naantali, so he could not buy any food on the boat. Therefore I invited him to eat with me. When we arrived in Sweden, he asked me to come to the vicarage outside Norrtälje. We had pleasant fellowship for the day, and then I proceeded on to Trollhättan and said goodbye to my mother. I advertised the car in the newspaper, it was only a few days left before I would go back, but already on the first day a missionary came in who needed to buy a car, he paid 3000 kronor, and I flew back to Australia.

Travel to Tumut

We used to buy cars at state auctions, where the vehicles were serviced and were usually not old. Irmeli participated in these auctions, and she sometimes became a little excited when we were bidding. When we wanted to make a bid, we had to raise our hand to indicate that we were making a bid. The auctioneer used to build the bids by a hundred dollar increments. There was a hundred dollars increase, every time we raised our hand. We were going to buy a passenger car this time, and Irmeli liked a particular car and wanted it. She would just look at it. It was I who laid the bids. But shortly after I raised my hand, Irmeli also raised her hand, and it became a two hundred dollar increase instead of one hundred dollars. It started itching in my head, and I scratched my head, and the auctioneer, though I made a bid, and he raised another hundred dollars. But we finally bought the car, for more than we bargained for.

We had bought another car after the theft of our bus. We found a Holden Twin Cab, which was a police car with an extra large tank. When this car was packed, I went down to Tumut for a business trip. When I was done, I would go to Wagga Wagga. Tumut is located in Snowy Mountain, a mountainous area with winding roads along the mountain slopes. You could drive about 100 km/h without any problems. Suddenly, a big kangaroo jumped up in front of the car, and then I remembered what the police told me in Roma when our van had burned up, he said that the bumper is like the strongest in the middle of the car, not the edges. On the left side of the road, there was a steep side down, and on the right side was the rock wall, I had no choice, so I focused on hitting the kangaroo in the middle of the car on the bumper. It was a massive kangaroo, maybe 100kg. And it was a mighty blow. I stopped and checked the "Roo Bar" (kangaroo bumper bar), and it was almost entirely without damage, except that it had moved a little closer to the grill. No car damage whatsoever. I didn't see the kangaroo. They usually continue to jump, even though they are hurt, and it is difficult to find them.

Irmeli fell in front of a truck

Irmeli had gone out in the evening in Allawah, where we stayed when I was on a business trip. She had a black top and a black skirt and had fallen from the pavement onto the road. Irmeli laid there on the road, a big truck came driving, and all of a sudden, the driver pulled into the curb and stopped. He said that he suddenly became fatigued and therefore the driver stopped the truck, and he had not seen Irmeli lying there in the black dress. But when he left the truck, he saw Irmeli lying there in her black clothes right in front of his front tyre. A few inches more and she would have been dead. Thank God, that He intervened and saved her life.

The sale of our company

We had been thinking of selling the company, and our auditor thought we should only sell the picture distribution business and keep the stainless steel and poster distribution. I had been wrestling for a long time with going back to Sweden and serving God in Sweden, but it had seemed awkward, and we had a colossal cheque credit with the bank. A lot of money was stuck with our customers and also the stock in our warehouse.

There had been three visiting preachers to our church in the last years that had pointed me out and asked me to come forward. They had prophesied over me, saying that I had a desire to return to my country and serve God there. But that my wife was not really for it. The last time this happened, Irmeli was in the church and heard it. I had used a broker to sell the company; they had gone through the finances and confirmed that the price for the company was excellent. But they failed to sell the company. So we took it off the market and waited on the Lord.

One Sunday after that, I went to church and went forward for prayer, then I prayed to the Lord this prayer "I just want to serve you, Lord". I did not ask for the company to be sold, which I had done for the last ten years. After six weeks a man called me from Queensland and asked if I wanted to sell the company. "Yes, I want to sell", I answered. He came down and signed the contract, and paid me the price for our company. Then he said he had to tell why he was buying the company. He said that six weeks ago, he got a strong urge to buy my company. I realised that it was at the same time when I was in the church at the altar. He called me but there was no answer, he rang periodically, but without a reply. He thought it had to be wrong, and stopped calling, but then he felt he had to keep calling and finally after these six weeks I answered the phone.

Selling our unit in Sydney.

We would also sell our apartment in Allawah. The local broker attempted, but nothing happened. We switched brokers and decided on an auction because then it would go fast. I went to the pastor and asked him to pray, then he said, "Curt, you just need one buyer". Next Sunday a brother came to me and said, "I have heard that you are going to sell the apartment and move to Sweden, how much are you asking for your unit". I told him, and then he said, "Curt, God is bigger than that, take my hand and agree with me about a higher price for your apartment"! Okay, I said. But I did not have the faith that he had, and I thought then that he would need to pull me up to his level of trust.
The day came for the public inspection of our unit, and the first couple that arrived said you must not sell this apartment to anyone else. We sold at the price that the broker had as a minimum. We had signed that the broker was allowed to sell at that amount if he wished. And it was $20,000 lower than what my brother in the Lord and I had agreed. But you can't believe what happened. You use a solicitor when you have to sell a property in Australia, the seller and the buyer both have their solicitors, and it can take weeks before they are ready with the documents and the title, to exchange contracts. When we changed the entire sales sum in the bank to Swedish krona, then the Swedish krona fell in value resulting in our receiving an additional $20,000 in profit. The exchange rate on Swedish krona had

fallen for only three or four days, and that was when we changed the currency in the bank. Perfect timing, totally outside our control, we had no idea about this beforehand.

We moved to Sweden on July 1, 2001, arrived on July 3 together with my mother-in-law Outi. Then I searched for a job and got a job as an editor and translator of the Christian Hillsong filmed services from Australia. It was fit for me, as I had attended church in Australia for the past 24 years, so it was like running water to translate with Swedish subtitles using the computer. These programs were broadcast over the Cable TV network in Västerås and Eskilstuna.

Later on, Kanal10 received these programs, which were broadcast via satellite across the Nordic countries. Here began a new chapter in our life that would lead to a more profound commitment to preaching Jesus in different parts of the world and also a greater involvement in Kanal 10, the Christian TV channel in Sweden, and in other countries. Right now, Kanal 10 has 5 TV stations worldwide.

Return to Sweden

Irmeli goes to be with the Lord

At 17th February 2017, Irmeli had the 9th operation at Sahlgrenska in Göteborg, by the same surgeon, that had operated her for the sixth time.
I went to the bakery to order a great cake so that we could celebrate our 50th wedding anniversary in the hospital on 18th February. Irmeli wanted to go on a cruise in the Caribbean later that year, to celebrate. Irmeli also had a heart murmur, which had worsened, and caused excess fluid to reside in her legs and her body. She went back to Västerås hospital to continue her rehabilitation. She was in and out of hospital until July. But she did not get any better. The heart problem was critical because the hip operation weakened her,

and he was not recommended to have surgery of the heart. I kept visiting her in the hospital every day for about seven hours. We always prayed when we met. At the end of June, she was on another visit to the hospital, but this time, the doctor would not let her go home, because her condition was terrible, and it was a struggle to breathe effortlessly. They kept her there, and I stayed with her until nightfall when I returned home.

When I closed the door to our flat, a great sorrow came over me, and I felt Irmeli was going to die, I was crying very much, but then I started to praise the Lord. After a while, I felt better. The following two weeks went by towards the end of the two weeks "as usual". In the end, Irmeli's condition seems to be better.

On 11th July, Irmeli called me, but I did not seem to have heard it, she left a message, and said, Good night Curt, I'm switching my phone off for the night. She always switched off her phone during the night. We had an appointment with the hip surgeon at 8 AM on 12th July. I was sitting on the ground floor in the waiting room. They were to help Irmeli to get down there, and Irmeli was expecting me. At 8 AM, a nurse rang me and said that Irmeli had passed away. I was in chock, and ran to the elevators, and came upon the 4th floor. The nurse opened the door to Irmeli's room, where Irmeli laid on the bed in total peace! Irmeli had gone to the Lord, at about 7 AM on the 12th July 2017.

I prayed for her to come back to life, but the Lord said to me, don't pray for her. I contacted Camilla and left a message for her to call me. Camilla came up to

Västerås, and we mourned Irmeli, but I knew that Irmeli is now with Jesus in heaven.

This is the saddest part of my life, when a true and wonderful partner in my life and a very dear wife, goes to the Lord after over 50 years of marriage.

Prayer of salvation!

It is my desire for you as the reader that you receive Jesus as your Saviour, as I did. I am writing down a prayer below. If you pray it and believe in your heart that God has raised Jesus from the dead, you will be saved.

That if thou shalt confess with thy mouth the Lord Jesus, and shalt believe in thine heart that God hath raised him from the dead, thou shalt be saved.
Romans 10:9 KJV

Prayer

Father in heaven, I come to you in the name of Jesus. I confess that I am a sinner. I have sinned against your commandments, and I ask you to forgive me for my sins. I accept that Jesus died on the cross for my sins and receive your salvation and forgiveness. I confess Jesus Christ as my personal Lord and Saviour. I thank you, Father, that you raised Jesus from the dead. Thank you, dear God, for hearing my prayer!

AMEN!

About the author

I am the son of the miller, Herman and Märta Larsson, born in Ulricehamn, Sweden. That is an area in Sweden where a lot of salespeople come from. A lot of textile factories are in the city of Borås, and the salespeople use to travel with a bicycle and have clothing with them, selling their wares to people in the countryside. I started to be interested in selling at an early age. But after my education, which was seven years in school, and a further three years of Industrial School, I was qualified as a turner and fitter. I never pursued this profession but went into selling just after my compulsory military exercise in the Swedish air force. After receiving Christ, I was an elder in the church in Australia.
Have also been working with the visiting ministry in prison in Sweden, for several years.

Lightning Source UK Ltd.
Milton Keynes UK
UKHW011047091221
395376UK00002B/302